The US Dollar and the BRICS Challenge –
Towards a new global financial order

The US Dollar and the BRICS Challenge –

Towards a new global financial order

"The value of money lies not in the coin or the bill,

but in the faith we place in it."

Ralph Waldo Emerso

Table of contents

Prolog

Continuous change and rapid technological progress raises the question of the stability of our future and of the global financial system. This book, "The US Dollar and the BRICS Challenge," addresses this issue in a comprehensive manner. It examines the historical dominance of the US dollar and sheds light on the emerging challenge posed by the BRICS countries (Brazil, Russia, India, China and South Africa), which are increasingly positioning themselves as a counterweight to the traditional economic power centers.

Since the introduction of the Bretton Woods system in 1944, the US dollar has played a central role in international trade and financial policy. The establishment of the dollar as the reserve currency created a foundation for decades of economic stability and growth, at least in the Western Hemisphere. But over time, cracks in this system began to become visible, particularly due to economic and political tensions, the financial crisis of 2008 and the steady increase in US national debt.

The BRICS countries have not only developed enormously economically over the past two decades, but have also gained political importance. With their considerable resources, large populations and growing markets, they are increasingly challenging the dominance of the established Western economic powers. Their ambition to promote a multipolar world order is reflected in the creation of new financial institutions such as the New Development Bank (NDB) and the Contingent Reserve Arrangement (CRA), which are designed as alternatives to the International Monetary Fund (IMF) and the World Bank.

This book analyses the economic and political strategies behind the rise of the BRICS countries and examines their potential impact on the future role of the US dollar in the global financial system. It highlights the various mechanisms and instruments that these countries use to strengthen their position on the world stage and reduce dependence on the dollar. It also examines in detail the role of trade agreements, investments in infrastructure and technology and the development of alternative payment systems.

Another central theme of this book is the examination of the geopolitical implications of a possible shift in global financial power. The competition between the USA and the BRICS countries is reflected not only in economic tensions, but also in security and diplomatic tensions. The question of whether a new world order in which the US dollar no longer plays the dominant role will lead to more stability or new conflicts is of utmost relevance.

This new edition takes into account current developments and data up to and including 2024 in order to paint the most precise picture of the current situation possible. Numerous expert interviews and case studies complement the theoretical analyses and provide insights into the practical implementation and challenges facing the BRICS countries.

I would like to thank all those who contributed to the creation of this book. Their commitment and expertise have made a significant contribution to making this work a well-founded and worthwhile analysis of global financial dynamics. My special thanks also go to the readers, whose interest and critical engagement with the contents of this book make a valuable contribution to the discussion about the future of our global financial system.

I hope that this book will not only help to clarify many questions, but also open up new perspectives and encourage people to continue to closely follow and question developments in the international financial world.

The BRICS summit took place in August 2023. The five BRICS states are still planning - so it is rumored - their own gold-based reserve currency. This rumor is supported by several events. The world is currently experiencing massive structural changes. NATO is expanding further eastwards and northwards in Europe. A direct consequence of NATO's eastward expansion is the military conflict in Ukraine. In Africa, more and more countries are fighting back against their former colonial powers. Military coups, such as in Niger and Gabon, are overthrowing civilian governments that conform to the West.

In addition, other oil-producing countries are joining the BRICS group on the occasion of the BRICS summit mentioned above. These include countries such as Argentina, Egypt, Ethiopia, Iran, Saudi Arabia and the United Arab Emirates. These countries plan to trade their oil in currencies other than the petrodollar. This would lead to a further weakening of the US dollar.

Russia has been excluded from the SWIFT system. For Russia, exclusion from the SWIFT system means that Russian banks can no longer communicate directly with other international banks to process cross-border transact-tions. Without access to the SWIFT network, Russia is cut off from most international payment and settlement systems. This could make trade with other countries more difficult and affect economic relations. Such isolation should destabilize Russian financial markets and reduce the confidence of investors. Exclusion from the SWIFT system is a serious measure and should be understood as a means of political pressure.

It is therefore not surprising that the rumor of a new reserve currency - possibly backed by the Yuan - is being fueled. Added to this is the apparently unsuccessful visit of the American Secretary of State Blinken to China. Immediately afterwards, the stock market value of the US dollar fell by several points. China holds immense dollar reserves due to its export surplus.

After that, former US Secretary of State Henry Kissinger visited China, of course privately and without any diplomatic mission.

Henry Kissinger, now 100 years old, is highly respected in China, mainly because of his role in normalizing relations between the United States and the People's Republic of China in the 1970s. As then US Secretary of State, he played a crucial role in the secret negotiations with Chinese leader Zhou Enlai.

It remains to be seen whether his visit can dissuade China and the BRICS countries from their financial plans. Russia and China are among the top four countries in the world when it comes to buying gold. Brazil increased its gold reserves by 53.75 tons in the second quarter of 2021, almost doubling its stocks. India is quite well represented with 787.40 tons of gold reserves and has acquired more than 150 tons in recent years.

China stores 2,010.51 tons of gold. The country is also the largest gold producer in the world, accounting for around twelve percent of global production. However, Russia has the largest gold reserves with 2,301.64 tons and has spent the equivalent of around 36 billion euros over the past five years to increase its reserves and thus be less dependent on the US dollar. This has even overtaken China. The Russian gold industry is worth billions, so not much gold even needs to be imported. The country's gold reserves rose by 6.22 tons in the third quarter of 2021. The BRICS countries can use this gold to become largely independent of the dollar.

China also holds immense dollar reserves. If China were to sell its immense dollar reserves, it would have a significant impact on the global economy and financial markets. Selling large amounts of US dollars would reduce the value of the dollar against other currencies due to an oversupply. A devaluation of the US dollar would have far-reaching effects on the international trading community, especially on countries that are heavily dependent on trade with the US. On the other hand, China is also dependent on the US, as it exports a large proportion of its goods to the US. A sudden devaluation of the US dollar could affect the competitiveness of Chinese exports, as they would become more expensive for US customers. This would have a negative impact on Chinese economic growth. Selling dollar reserves could therefore also result in losses for China if the dollar depreciates during the sale.

However, the global economy is a complex network that is influenced by various actors and circumstances. In recent decades, the dominance of the US dollar as the world reserve currency has played an important role. The dollar has shaped the international trade landscape for many decades and has had a significant impact on geopolitical relations. But in recent years, new powers have risen and challenged the status quo. The BRICS countries - Brazil, Russia, India, China and South Africa - have gained increasing economic importance and are pushing for reform of the international financial system.

My book "The US Dollar and the BRICS Challenge" aims to bring readers closer to the history of dollar dominance and the emerging BRICS countries as a possible counterweight. It is intended to be seen as an attempt to shed light on current events in the world and thus help to better understand the current upheavals and restructuring. The book sheds light on the background that led to the power struggles of this time and it takes a look into a possible future to analyze the effects on the global economy. It will examine the various aspects of the topic, from the historical events that led to the emergence of dollar dominance to the current efforts of the BRICS countries to escape this dominance and strengthen their own position.

We will examine the roots of dollar dominance. From the Bretton Woods Conference in 1944 to the abolition of the gold standard in 1971, the key milestones on the way to the global acceptance of the dollar as a reserve currency will be covered. The role of the United States as a superpower and its economic and political interest in maintaining dollar dominance will also be questioned.

Another part of the book is devoted to the BRICS countries and their rise as economic heavyweights. Each country is considered individually to analyze its specific economic, political and social developments. All five countries have different challenges and opportunities, but all strive to have their own voice in the global economic order. Their efforts to build alternative currency and financial structures will also be examined in detail.

In addition, the conflicts and tensions between the US dollar and the BRICS countries are examined in more detail. I want to show how the United States is defending its dominance in the world economy by all means and is taking measures to maintain the status of the dollar. At the same time, the BRICS countries are forming their own economic alliance and are looking for ways to escape dependence on the dollar. This struggle for power and influence has an impact on global stability and will possibly lead to a redesign of the international financial architecture.

Furthermore, a look ahead is given. What might the world economy look like in the next few decades? What role do the BRICS countries and the dollar play? What scenarios are conceivable and how might they affect the various players? These questions are discussed on the basis of current developments and trends, with both optimistic and pessimistic scenarios being examined.

It is important to point out that this book cannot provide definitive answers. The dynamics between the US dollar and the BRICS countries are too complex and multi-faceted, and developments are still ongoing. Rather, this book aims to encourage people to think about the current world order and the possible changes that directly affect each and every one of us. This book offers a wealth of information, analyses and perspectives that enable the reader to form their own opinion and stimulate further discussions.

The dominance of the dollar and the emerging BRICS states are a topic that concerns not only economic and financial experts, but all of us. The decisions that will be made in the coming years could have a lasting impact on the global economy and realign geopolitical relations. It is up to us to understand these developments and to participate actively in them. It is up to us to connect the connections between the current events that directly affect and surround us with these global events. We must understand that current developments in politics and the economy are directly related to the struggles between the two opponents.

This book is an invitation to deal with this topic and take a look behind the scenes of the global economy.

It is an invitation to discover the history, present and future of dollar dominance and the BRICS states. It is important to me to invite you to immerse yourself with me in this world, which is full of challenges, opportunities and uncertain prospects. Decisions that could be made by the two opponents in this regard affect each and every one of us directly - so we should strive to understand them, discuss them and, if necessary, influence them.

Hermann Selchow

The shifts in power relations caused by the BRICS Countries

Over the past few decades, global power relations have changed dramatically. These shifts have been largely driven by the economic and political rise of the BRICS countries: Brazil, Russia, India, China, and South Africa. These nations have not only increased their economic power, but have also significantly expanded their political and cultural influence on a global scale. This chapter examines the various facets of these power shifts and analyzes the long-term implications for the global order.

The BRICS group emerged as a concept in the early 2000s and was popularized by British economist Jim O'Neill. Originally known as BRIC before South Africa joined in 2010, this group of emerging economies symbolized the potential for strong economic growth outside the traditionnal Western powers. The emergence of the BRICS countries marks the beginning of a new era in which economic dominance is no longer held exclusively by the G7 nations.

The economic strength of the BRICS countries has increaseed significantly over the past two decades. China and India are experiencing impressive growth rates and are now among the largest economies in the world. Russia's vast reserves of natural resources, Brazil's agricultural capabilities and South Africa's role as a gateway to Africa complement this economic potential.

China has established itself as the world's second largest economy and aims to overtake the US in the foreseeable future. The Belt and Road Initiative (BRI) is a clear sign of China's ambition to expand its economic and geopolitical reach. By building infrastructure in Asia, Africa and Europe, China is promoting international trade and cementing its position as a global economic leader.

India, with its young population and dynamic IT industry, is another important player within the BRICS. The Indian economy has grown significantly through reforms and increasing integration into the global economy. Initiatives such as Make in India and the Digital India campaign demonstrate India's ambition to become a central player on the global stage.

Brazil and South Africa also play essential roles within the BRICS group. Brazil is a leading exporter of agricultural products and has rich natural resources. South Africa, on the other hand, acts as the economic center of Africa and has significant natural resources that are important to the global economy.

Russia uses its vast energy resources to exert economic and political influence. As one of the world's largest producers of oil and gas, Russia has a strategic position, especially in energy relations with Europe and Asia.

The BRICS countries have refined their political strategies to better represent their interests on the global stage. Joint diplomatic initiatives and the building of alternative institutions to Western-dominated organizations show that these countries want to use their collective power.

The regular BRICS summits provide a platform for coordination and cooperation on political, economic and social issues. These meetings promote dialogue and unity among member states and help develop a common vision for the future.

With the establishment of the New Development Bank (NDB) and the Contingent Reserve Arrangement (CRA), the BRICS countries have begun to create alternative financial structures to traditional Western institutions such as the International Monetary Fund (IMF) and the World Bank. These new institutions aim to promote economic development and ensure financial stability in member countries.

In addition to their economic and political power, the BRICS countries also have significant cultural and social influences. Through the export of culture and technology and exchanges in education and science, these countries contribute to globalization and shape the cultural landscapes worldwide.

Initiatives such as the China-Africa Cooperation Forum and the India-Africa Forum Summit promote cultural exchanges and cooperation in education and research. These programs help foster mutual understanding and respect between nations and build long-term relationships.

The BRICS countries invest heavily in research and development and promote innovation in areas such as information technology, biotechnology and renewable energy. Indian IT companies, Chinese tech giants and Russian space programs are examples of the leading roles these countries play in the global innovation landscape.

The increasing power of the BRICS countries has far-reaching implications for the global order. These nations are challenging the dominance of traditional Western powers and are working to create a multipolar world in which multiple centers of power exist.

The BRICS countries aspire to a multipolar world order in which power and influence are more evenly distributed. This vision contrasts with the unipolar dominance of the United States after the Cold War and the bipolar world during the Cold War. A multipolar world order could lead to more balanced and fair global governance.

The growing strength of the BRICS countries brings both challenges and opportunities. On the one hand, the shift in the balance of power could lead to tensions and conflicts as existing powers seek to defend their dominance. On the other hand, it offers new opportunities for cooperation and solving global problems through a diversified power structure.

In addition to their economic interests, the BRICS countries also pursue a number of political goals aimed at strengthening their global position and protecting their sovereignty and interests. These policy goals include both domestic and foreign policy dimensions and are closely linked to the group's economic aspirations.

A key policy goal of the BRICS countries is to strengthen their national sovereignty and independence from Western influences and institutions. These states strive to establish a multipolar world order in which they are not dependent on the dominant Western powers. This is evident, for example, in their criticism of the existing international financial institutions such as the International Monetary Fund (IMF) and the World Bank, which are seen as instruments of Western dominance.

The BRICS countries actively promote a multipolar world order based on the principle of equality and mutual respect. They argue that such an order is necessary to ensure a fairer distribution of power and resources. This goal is evident in their support for the reform of the United Nations, particularly the UN Security Council, to promote more representative and democratic global governance.

Another policy goal of the BRICS group is to promote regional stability and security. This is achieved through diplomatic initiatives and support for peace processes in various regions. For example, the BRICS countries are involved in Africa through various development and peace initiatives aimed at resolving conflicts and promoting economic development. In Asia, too, they play an important role in stabilizing and developing conflict areas.

Combating terrorism and extremism is a common concern among the BRICS countries. These countries are often targets of terrorist activities and see security cooperation as necessary to combat these threats. Through joint security agreements and the sharing of information and technology, they work to improve their capabilities to combat terrorism and extremism.

Although the BRICS countries have different political systems and views on human rights and democracy, they emphasize the importance of these principles in their international relations. They argue that the promotion of human rights and democracy should not be achieved through external pressure, but through dialogue and mutual respect. This stance often contrasts with Western approaches that favor sanctions and intervention.

The BRICS countries seek to expand their diplomatic networks and alliances to strengthen their global position. By developing bilateral and multilateral relations with other emerging economic powers and developing countries, they seek to create a counterweight to Western dominance. These diplomatic efforts also include support for regional organizations such as the African Union (AU), the Commonwealth of Independent States (CIS), and the South Asian Association for Regional Cooperation (SAARC).

Sustainable development is another key policy objective of the BRICS countries. They emphasize the need to balance economic growth with social and environmental goals. This is evident in their support for international agreements such as the Paris Climate Agreement and their own national initiatives to promote renewable energy, reduce poverty, and improve education and healthcare.

In addition to their economic interests, the BRICS countries also pursue a number of policy objectives aimed at strengthening their global position and promoting a multipolar world order. These policy objectives are diverse and range from strengthening national sovereignty and independence to promoting regional stability and security to combating terrorism and extremism. By expanding diplomatic networks and promoting sustainable development, the BRICS countries are working to create a fairer and more balanced global order in which their voices and interests are adequately represented.

The United States, as the traditionally dominant global power, has closely monitored the development and strengthening of the BRICS countries. The US has responded to these new geopolitical realities in different ways, which is evident at various levels from diplomatic efforts to economic measures to military strategies.

The US has increased its diplomatic efforts to consolidate its traditional alliances and forge new partnerships. This is evident in intensive cooperation with the European Union, NATO, and strategic partners in Asia, such as Japan, South Korea, and India. Particularly noteworthy is the so-called "Indo-Pacific Strategy," which aims to position the US as a central power in the Asia-Pacific region and limit China's influence.

Economically, the US has taken measures to increase its competitiveness and erect trade barriers against BRICS countries. The trade conflict between the US and China is a prominent example of how economic power is used to pursue geopolitical goals. Through tariffs and trade restrictions, the US seeks to limit Chinese exports and protect American companies.

In addition, the US is actively seeking new trade agreements that promote its economic interests while reducing its dependence on BRICS countries. The recently renewed NAFTA agreement, now known as USMCA (United States-Mexico-Canada Agreement), is an example of these efforts.

Militarily, the US has increased its presence in critical regions and developed new defense strategies to counter potential threats from BRICS countries. Particularly in Asia, the US has strengthened its military alliances and increase-ed its troop presence in strategic areas such as the South China Sea. This serves both as a deterrent and to secure trade routes and geopolitical interests.

Modernizing the armed forces and developing new technologies, including cyber defense and space defense, are also essential components of the American strategy to maintain its military superiority.

However, the shift in the balance of power also carries the risk of military conflict, especially in areas of high geopolitical tension. There is an increased risk of military clashes in the South China Sea, where several countries, including China, have territorial claims. The US has made it clear that it will defend freedom of navigation in these waters, which could lead to confrontations with China.

But there is also the potential for conflict in Eastern Europe, where Russia has expanded its military presence. NATO has increased its forces in Eastern Europe in response to Russia's actions in Ukraine and other areas, increasing tensions in the region.

To avoid military conflict, the US is also relying on preventive diplomacy and dialogue. High-level meetings and talks between the US and BRICS countries, especially China and Russia, are crucial to avoid misunderstandings and find common solutions to global challenges.

Despite the rivalry and competition, there are also areas where the US and BRICS countries work together. Global challenges such as climate change, terrorism and combating pandemics require multilateral cooperation. This presents opportunities for dialogue and cooperation that can help reduce tensions and pursue common interests.

The US response to the growing power of the BRICS countries is complex and multifaceted, characterized by a mix of diplomatic, economic and military strategies. While the risk of military conflict remains, the US is also working to address common global challenges through diplomacy and cooperation. The future of international relations will depend largely on how successful these strategies are and how well they succeed in ensuring peaceful coexistence in an increasingly multipolar world order.

The exit from the Petrodollar and its impact on world trade

The petrodollar, a term that refers to the U.S. dollar used in international oil trading, has long played a central role in the global financial system. This practice became established in the 1970s when the U.S. and Saudi Arabia reached an agreement to trade oil in U.S. dollars. However, in recent years, several countries have taken steps to move away from the petrodollar. This has significant implications for world trade and the global financial system.

The move away from the petrodollar is due to several factors. First, many countries are looking for ways to reduce their dependence on the U.S. dollar and the geopolitical risks associated with it. The U.S. use of sanctions that limit access to U.S. dollar transactions has prompted countries such as Russia and Iran to seek alternatives.

Second, economic and political tensions between the U.S. and emerging powers such as China have led to moves to conduct trade in other currencies. China, as the world's largest oil importer, has started trading oil in yuan to strengthen its currency internationally and reduce dependence on the US dollar.

The exit from the petrodollar has far-reaching consequences for global trade. First of all, it leads to a diversification of trading currencies. Countries that use alternative currencies for oil trading encourage the use of their own currencies or other major currencies such as the euro, the yuan or even cryptocurrencies. This contributes to the emergence of a multipolar monetary system that weakens the dominance of the US dollar.

Such a system can change global trade dynamics by encouraging new trade relationships and partnerships. Countries that move away from the petrodollar could build closer economic ties with each other, leading to greater economic integration and cooperation.

The move away from the petrodollar could also lead to increased volatility in the global financial system. The US dollar has long served as a stable reserve currency, and its dominance has helped stabilize international trade. However, diversification of trading currencies could lead to short-term uncertainty as markets need to adapt to new trading and monetary practices.

However, in the long term, a multipolar monetary system could contribute to a more stable and balanced global economy. It could reduce the risk associated with dependence on a single currency and increase resilience to economic shocks.

The shift away from the petrodollar also has significant geopolitical implications. Countries that use alternative currencies for trade gain political and economic independence. This could lead to a shift in the geopolitical balance of power as the US's ability to exert its influence through financial sanctions is limited.

At the same time, new alliances and partnerships based on shared economic interests could emerge. The BRICS countries play a central role here as they are actively working to create an alternative financial system. By promoting trade in their own currencies and supporting initiatives such as the New Development Bank, they are helping to create a multipolar world order.

The shift to a diversified monetary system brings both challenges and opportunities. For many countries, adapting to new trading currencies presents logistical and economic challenges. The need to hold and manage foreign exchange reserves in multiple currencies could add additional costs and complexity.

On the other hand, diversifying trading currencies offers the opportunity to reduce economic dependence and achieve greater financial autonomy. This could be particularly beneficial for developing countries seeking to strengthen their economic sovereignty and improve their integration into the global economy.

The phase-out of the petrodollar and the associated changes in global trade have profound implications for the global financial system. The shift toward a multipolar monetary system could lead to a more balanced and resilient global economy, but it also brings short-term challenges and uncertainties. While the US adapts its strategies to respond to these changes, the BRICS countries and other emerging powers will continue to play a central role in shaping the new world order.

Reasons for oil-producing countries to join BRICS

Diversification of economic partnerships: Oil-producing countries, particularly those in the Middle East such as Saudi Arabia and the United Arab Emirates, want to diversify their economic relationships to avoid being solely dependent on Western markets. BRICS membership gives them access to new markets and investment opportunities in the growing economies of BRICS members such as China and India.

Geopolitical strategies: The geopolitical landscape has changed dramatically in recent years. Countries such as Russia and China offer alternatives to traditional Western alliances. Oil-producing countries are looking for ways to strengthen their geopolitical position and reduce their dependence on Western states, especially in the face of political tensions and economic sanctions.

Economic and financial benefits: BRICS countries offer potential economic and financial benefits through joint development banks and investment funds. These entities can finance projects in infrastructure, technology and other key areas, which is particularly attractive to oil-producing countries seeking to diversify and modernize their economies.

Political independence and sovereignty: By joining a bloc like BRICS, oil-producing countries can strengthen their political independence and sovereignty. They can free themselves from Western political and economic pressure and form alternative alliances that better suit their national interests.

Common interests: Many BRICS and oil-producing countries share common interests in areas such as energy, infrastructure development and economic cooperation. These common interests can form the basis for closer cooperation and mutual support.

Growing markets in BRICS countries: BRICS countries represent some of the largest and fastest-growing economies in the world. Oil-producing countries see this as an opportunity to expand their export market and capitalize on the growing demand for energy in these countries.

Overall, oil-producing countries are looking for ways to expand their economic base, strengthen their geopolitical position and gain more independence in the international arena. Membership in BRICS offers an attractive way to achieve these goals.

The BRICS countries are therefore playing a crucial role in reshaping the global balance of power. Their growing economic, political and cultural strength has the potential to fundamentally change the world order. While these changes bring both challenges and opportunities, the future of the global order remains uncertain. However, it is clear that the BRICS countries will continue to play a significant role in the coming decades and significantly influence the global economy and politics.

The challenge of US-Dollar dominance

The global financial landscape is shaped by one dominant currency - the US dollar. Since the end of World War II, the dollar has maintained its position as the world's reserve currency and has had a significant impact on international trade, financial markets and geopolitical relations. But in recent years, more and more voices have been raised to discuss the challenges and risks of dollar dominance.

The dollar's rise to become the world's accepted reserve currency began after World War II with the introduction of the Bretton Woods system. In this system, most global currencies were pegged to the dollar, which in turn was pegged to gold. This link to gold gave the dollar stability and trust, making it the preferred currency for international transactions. But the Bretton Woods system collapsed in the 1970s when the US abandoned its gold peg and the dollar became a freely floating currency.

Despite the collapse of the Bretton Woods system, the dollar maintained its dominance as a reserve currency. This was partly due to the strong American economy and the strong political influence of the US in the world. In addition, many countries have chosen the dollar as an anchor currency to stabilize their own currency and instill confidence in their economy. This resulted in the majority of global foreign exchange reserves being held in dollars and the dollar dominating international trade.

However, there are increasing concerns and criticisms about dollar dominance. One reason for this is the high dependence of the global economy on the dollar. Since the dollar is the main trading currency, many countries are forced to hold large amounts of dollar reserves to maintain their trading activities. This dependence on a single currency poses risks, especially when the US makes political or economic decisions that could threaten the stability of the dollar.

Another problem is the US's unilateral decision-making power over the sanctions and embargoes it can impose on other countries. Since the dollar is widely used as an international reserve currency, the US can restrict other countries' access to the global financial system by denying them access to the dollar. This has far-reaching implications for the countries affected and can lead to economic turmoil and political tensions.

In addition, the US's expansionary monetary policy has raised concerns in recent years. Through its low interest rate policy and quantitative easing program, the US has pumped large amounts of dollars into the global economy. This has flooded global markets with dollar liquidity and may have contributed to financial imbalances and speculative bubbles.

In the face of these challenges, some countries are looking for alternatives to the dollar. China, for example, has strengthened the international role of the Chinese yuan and has tried to establish the yuan as an alternative reserve currency. Russia and other emerging countries have reduced their dollar reserves and invested more in other currencies and gold to reduce their dependence on the dollar.

In addition, there are also efforts to use digital currencies such as Bitcoin or other cryptocurrencies as an alternative to the dollar. These decentralized digital currencies offer new opportunities for cross-border transactions and could challenge traditional currencies in the future.

It remains to be seen how the challenge to dollar dominance will develop. The US still has a strong economy and the advantage of the widespread use of the dollar. Nevertheless, discussions and efforts to achieve greater diversity and stability in the global financial system cannot be overlooked. The future of dollar dominance depends on many factors, including economic developments, geopolitical changes and the willingness of countries to accept alternative currencies.

Overall, the challenge of dollar dominance is a complex issue that continues to be intensely debated. Dependence on a single currency poses risks and uncertainties for the stability of global financial markets. The search for alternatives and efforts to achieve greater diversity in the international monetary system are an important step towards a more resilient and balanced global economic order. It is to be hoped that these discussions will lead to positive changes in a more balanced balance of power and lay the foundation for a more stable and sustainable global financial system.

The discussion of challenging the dollar's dominance also has implications for the geopolitical landscape. Some countries, especially those affected by US sanctions, are looking for ways to bypass the dollar and create alternative trade routes. This has led to the emergence of new economic alliances and initiatives aimed at reducing the dollar's dominance.

A notable example of this is China's establishment of the Asian Infrastructure Investment Bank (AIIB) in 2015. The

AIIB is designed to serve as an alternative to the World Bank and finance projects in Asia. China has also increased its efforts to enter into bilateral trade agreements and conduct international trade in yuan. These measures are aimed at reducing the dollar's influence in the region and strengthening the role of the yuan.

There are also efforts at the international level to reduce dependence on the dollar. One example of this is the establishment of the BRICS bloc, consisting of Brazil, Russia, India, China and South Africa. These emerging economies have increased their efforts to conduct trade in their own currencies, thus reducing the influence of the dollar. In addition, they have made proposals for a new global reserve currency to increase the stability of the international financial system.

The European Union had also discussed the possibility of strengthening the euro as an alternative to the dollar in the past. As the world's second-largest reserve currency, the euro could have played a larger role in international financial markets, thus challenging the dominance of the dollar. The EU had taken initial steps to promote the euro as a trading currency and to reduce the use of the dollar in certain sectors. These plans were hampered and complicated by interventions of various kinds. Internal rivalries between EU member states, as well as the economic interests of major European industry, played a role.

It is important to note, however, that challenging dollar dominance is not without obstacles. The dominance of the dollar is based on a variety of factors, including the size and strength of the American economy, the depth of financial markets, and the trustworthiness of the dollar as a reserve currency. It will not be easy to shake or replace this dominance.

There are also concerns about possible alternatives to the dollar. While the rise of cryptocurrencies such as Bitcoin has attracted attention, they still come with significant volatility and uncertainty. It is questionable whether they will be able to offer the stability and trustworthiness of an established reserve currency such as the dollar in the near future.

Overall, the challenge to dollar dominance remains an issue with far-reaching implications for global economics and politics. The discussions and efforts to promote greater diversity in the international monetary system are important to promote the stability and sustainability of global financial markets. It will be interesting to see how this dynamic develops in the coming years and whether it succeeds in challenging the dollar's dominance.

The Emergence of the BRICS Countries

The BRICS are a group of emerging economies that play a significant role in the global arena. The term "BRICS" was first coined in 2001 by economist Jim O'Neill to describe four emerging economies: Brazil, Russia, India and China. Later, South Africa was added to the group and it received its official name BRICS. The emergence of these states as a political and economic force has an interesting history, which we will now examine in more detail.

Brazil, the largest country in South America, played a central role in the creation of the BRICS. In the 1990s, Brazil was in an economic crisis characterized by high inflation, corruption and social inequality. The country was looking for ways to diversify its economy and become internationally competitive. In 2001, Brazil took the initiative and invited Russia, India and China to a meeting to discuss economic cooperation.

Russia, the world's largest country, found itself in a similar situation to Brazil after the collapse of the Soviet Union in the 1990s. Its economy suffered from a severe recession and political stability was at risk. Russia was looking for new ways to exploit its resources and rebuild its economy. Brazil's invitation to the meeting was a welcome opportunity for Russia to strengthen its economic and political ties with other emerging markets.

India, the world's second most populous country, also had the goal of modernising its economy and becoming globally competitive. The country saw cooperation with other emerging economies as a way to better represent its interests and increase its influence in the global economy.

Brazil's invitation provided India with an opportunity to create a platform for exchanging ideas and experiences and to explore possible areas of cooperation.

China, the world's most populous country, had already started liberalising its economy and opening itself to foreign investment in the 1980s. The country aimed to consolidate its position as a world leader in manufacturing and exporting. The invitation from Brazil was of interest to China as it would provide new markets for its products and strengthen its political and economic role on the global stage.

These four countries recognized the common challenges and opportunities they faced and decided to join forces. The meeting in Brazil in 2001 marked the beginning of a new era of cooperation between the emerging economies. Various mechanisms and platforms were created to promote the exchange of ideas, trade and investment.

In the following years, cooperation between the BRICS countries developed steadily. They established the New Development Bank, which was intended to serve as an alternative to the established international financial institutions. The BRICS countries also began to intensify their cooperation in the fields of education, science and technology, energy and culture.

The decision to admit South Africa as a member in 2010 was another important step in the development of the BRICS countries. South Africa was the largest African country and was chosen for its economic potential and geopolitical importance. The inclusion of South Africa strengthened the position of the BRICS as representatives of emerging markets and gave them a greater voice in global affairs.

The BRICS have grown over time into a significant political and economic force, representing more than 40% of the world's population and about a quarter of global economic output. Cooperation among the BRICS has helped promote the development of member countries and strengthen their voice in international institutions such as the United Nations.

The emergence of the BRICS was a result of the founding members' shared vision and commitment. By working together, they have created a platform to promote their interests and find common solutions to global challenges. The BRICS have become a major player in global politics and economics and are expected to continue to play a growing role in the future.

The BRICS have continued to expand their cooperation in recent years and strengthen their position in the global economy.

One of the main goals of the BRICS countries was to challenge the dominance of the western industrialized nations in the global financial architecture. To this end, they created the New Development Bank (NDB) to support infrastructure projects and sustainable development in the BRICS countries and other emerging economies. The NDB provides an alternative to the World Bank and other established development institutions and helps to strengthen economic cooperation among the BRICS countries.

Another important tool for cooperation is the BRICS Summit, which takes place annually and offers the heads of state and government of the member countries the opportunity to strengthen their bilateral relations and discuss joint projects. The BRICS Summit has become an important forum to discuss political issues of common interest and to promote cooperation in areas such as trade, investment, technology, culture and education.

Economically, the BRICS countries have experienced impressive growth in recent years. China has now become the world's second-largest economy and has assumed a significant role in global trade and manufacturing. India is also experiencing strong economic growth and has become a major player in information technology and outsourcing. Brazil and Russia have faced economic challenges but have made progress in certain areas such as energy, mining and agriculture. South Africa has capitalised on its potential as a gateway to the African continent and established a growing role as a trading partner and investment destination.

The BRICS have also increased their cooperation on political affairs. They often share similar views on global issues such as United Nations Security Council reform and combating terrorism. By adopting common positions in international forums such as the United Nations, the BRICS are seeking to strengthen their voice and exert greater influence in shaping global policy.

The BRICS, however, also face challenges. There are signifycant differences in economic structure, political systems and levels of social development within the group. The member countries face various internal and external challenges such as corruption, inequality, infrastructure deficiencies and trade barriers. The BRICS countries must address these challenges to ensure their long-term cooperation and sustainable growth.

Another important point when considering the BRICS countries is their role as an emerging power in the global south. The BRICS countries have increasingly expanded their cooperation with other emerging and developing countries in recent years. They have launched initiatives such as the BRICS Plus format, in which representatives of other emerging countries and regional organizations are invited to the BRICS summits. This expanded cooperation is intended to help strengthen the voice of the emerging economies in international affairs and promote south-south cooperation. The aim is also to reduce the influence of the dollar and replace it with their own system.

Overall, the BRICS countries have undergone remarkable development in recent years. They have become an influential political and economic force, creating a platform to promote their interests and find common solutions to global challenges. The BRICS have demonstrated that emerging economies can play a significant role in the global economy and that cooperation and dialogue are the keys to promoting growth and stability.

It is important to note that the future of the BRICS depends on many factors, including the implementation of reforms, overcoming internal challenges and the ability to adapt to a rapidly changing global landscape. Nevertheless, the BRICS have proven their ability to work together as a group and pursue their common goals. Their emergence and development represent a significant development in global politics and economics and will undoubtedly continue to be of interest.

The establishment of the BRICS was based on a number of economic and political reasons that prompted member countries to intensify their cooperation.

Economic reasons played a crucial role in the creation of the BRICS countries. The member countries recognized the enormous economic potential that could be created by combining their resources, markets and workforce. By joining forces, they wanted to strengthen their negotiating position in the global economy and increase their influence on international trade and financial rules.

China was already known as the "workshop of the world" at that time due to its large labor supply and competitive production costs. Brazil, Russia and India had abundant natural resources such as oil, gas, metals and agricultural commodities. By expanding economic cooperation, these resources could be used more efficiently to meet the needs of the member countries and other emerging economies.

In addition, the BRICS countries recognized the importance of market access and trade facilitation for their respective economies. By expanding trade within the group and promoting free trade, they were able to diversify their export markets and become more independent from traditional Western markets. China and India in particular were looking for new sales markets for their products and services.

Another economic reason for the creation of the BRICS was the need for greater cooperation in financing infrastructure projects and developing new financial instruments. The member countries recognized the challenges they faced in financing large projects and decided to create the New Development Bank (NDB). The NDB was to serve as a financing institution that supports infrastructure and development projects in the BRICS and other emerging economies. The creation of the NDB was a clear sign that the BRICS wanted to have their own voice in the global financial architecture.

Political reasons also played an important role in the creation of the BRICS. The member countries were aware that their voice was often not adequately considered in international affairs. They saw the BRICS platform as an opportunity to better represent their interests and have a greater influence on shaping global policy.

A key political goal of the BRICS was to challenge the dominance of Western industrialized nations in international institutions such as the United Nations, the International Monetary Fund (IMF), and the World Bank. They argued that these institutions were not sufficiently representative and democratic, and that their decisions often favored the interests of developed countries. By establishing the BRICS, they sought to strengthen their own voice and create alternative platforms for the exchange of ideas and political dialogue.

The BRICS also saw an opportunity to use their cooperation to promote peace, stability, and security in the world. They emphasized the importance of multilateralism and diplomacy in addressing global challenges such as climate change, terrorism, and nuclear non-proliferation. By adopting common positions on these issues, the BRICS sought to amplify their voices and promote their own vision of a fairer and more balanced world order.

The economic and political reasons for establishing the BRICS were closely intertwined. The member countries recognized that a strong economic base is a prerequisite for political influence and international recognition. By strengthening their economic cooperation, they could advance their political agenda and better represent their interests in global affairs.

The BRICS states also recognized the importance of strong political cooperation to effectively promote their economic interests. They sought to intensify their political relations, strengthen political dialogue, and develop common positions on international issues. This would enable them to act as a group and strengthen their negotiating position with other states and international organizations.

Another political reason for the establishment of the BRICS states was to create a counterweight to the existing power structures in global politics. The member countries saw cooperation as a way to unite their voices and advance common interests. In particular, China and Russia, which were viewed as emerging superpowers, were looking for a platform to expand their political and economic power on the international stage.

The BRICS also stressed the importance of sovereignty and non-interference in the internal affairs of other countries. They pursued a policy of equality and respect for the territorial integrity of all states. By building their cooperation on these principles, the BRICS sought to advance their own vision of a multipolar world order.

Another political aspect of the BRICS was their role as representatives of the emerging economies of the global South. The member countries saw themselves as a voice for the interests of developing countries and sought ways to strengthen South-South cooperation. Through their cooperation, they sought to create a balance between North and South and ensure that the voices of developing countries are heard in global affairs.

The BRICS have made great progress in their economic and political cooperation in recent years. They have expanded their trade relations, initiated joint investment projects and promoted the exchange of technology, education and culture. Their political coordination has also increased and they have adopted common positions at international forums such as the United Nations.

However, it is important to note that the BRICS countries also face some challenges. There are still differences in their political systems, economic structures and social development levels. It is often challenging to find consensus and make decisions that take into account the different interests of member countries. The BRICS countries need to continuously work on their internal cooperation and develop mechanisms to deal with disagreements and find common solutions.

In addition, the BRICS countries face external challenges such as the rise of protectionism and the volatility of global markets. These factors have affected the economic and political outlook of the BRICS countries and require adaptation and flexibility.

Despite these challenges, however, the BRICS countries remain committed to developing their cooperation and pursuing their common goals. They have shown that emerging economies can play a significant role in global politics and economics. The establishment of the BRICS countries was a milestone in the development of emerging markets and has the potential to influence the global order in a sustainable and equitable way.

The economic potential of the BRICS Countries

The BRICS countries, originally consisting of the founding countries Brazil, Russia, India, China and South Africa, are a group of emerging economies that have become increasingly important in recent years. These countries are characterized by their large populations, rich natural resources and high economic growth. In this text, we will take a close look at the economic potential of the BRICS countries and analyze how they are developing into important players in the global economy.

Brazil

Brazil, the largest country in South America, has one of the largest economies in the world. With its rich natural resources, such as oil, gas, minerals and agricultural products, Brazil has enormous economic potential. The agricultural industry in particular plays a significant role in the Brazilian economy. The country is one of the largest producers of soy, coffee, sugar and beef. In addition, Brazil has an emerging IT industry and is a major producer of motor vehicles. Despite these promising prospects, however, the country also faces challenges such as high inequality, corruption and complex bureaucracy.

Russia

Russia is the largest country in the world and plays a crucial role in the BRICS countries. With its extensive oil and gas reserves, Russia is one of the largest energy exporters in the world. This has given the country a strong position in international markets and driven its economy.

In addition, Russia has a wide range of industries, such as mechanical engineering, chemicals and the defense industry. Another economic potential of Russia lies in its education sector, which produces highly qualified specialists. However, Russia also faces challenges such as political instability, sanctions and a dependence on raw material exports.

India

India, with its huge population of over a billion people, has enormous economic potential. The country is characterized by a young and growing population, which generates a large demand for consumer goods and services. India is a leading producer of textiles, pharmaceutical products, information technology and IT services. The IT industry in India in particular has developed strongly in recent decades and has made a significant contribution to economic growth. Nevertheless, India faces challenges such as poverty, infrastructure deficiencies and complex regulation.

China

China is undoubtedly the largest player among the BRICS nations and has become one of the largest economies in the world. The country has benefited from its large workforce, low production costs and growing domestic market demand. China is a leading manufacturer of consumer goods, electronics, textiles and machinery. In particular, the technology sector in China, with companies such as Alibaba, Tencent and Huawei, is of international importance. In addition, China has made massive investments in renewable energy and is a leader in the solar power and electric vehicle industries. However, the country faces challenges such as pollution, rising labor costs and tensions in global trade.

South Africa

South Africa is the smallest country among the BRICS nations but plays an important role in the African economy. The country is rich in natural resources such as gold, diamonds and platinum and has a well-developed mining industry. In addition, South Africa has a strong financial industry and is a major player in the African banking sector. The country has a diverse industry that includes automobile production, chemicals, information technology and tourism. Despite this economic potential, South Africa faces challenges such as high unemployment, social inequality and structural problems in the areas of education and health.

Challenges to the dominance of the US-Dollar

The rise of the BRICS and their economic potential will of course have an impact on the dominance of the dollar as the world's reserve currency. The BRICS are striving to position their own currencies more strongly internationally and reduce the influence of the dollar. This could potentially affect the current situation of the global financial system and pose a challenge to the dominance of the dollar.

International payments and trade: A rise of the BRICS would lead to an increase in trade and payments in their own currencies. This would reduce the need for dollar transactions and reduce dependence on the US currency. China in particular has already made efforts to establish the renminbi as an international trading currency and has concluded bilateral currency swap agreements with various countries to promote the use of the renminbi in trade.

Reserve currencies: The BRICS also aim to make their currencies more attractive as reserve currencies. Currently, the majority of the world's currency reserves are held in US dollars. If the BRICS can strengthen their own currencies and build confidence, they could provide an alternative to dollar reserves and promote the diversification of global foreign exchange reserves.

Development of financial institutions: The BRICS have established their own financial institutions to promote their economic cooperation and strengthen their position in the global financial architecture. One example is the

BRICS' establishment of the New Development Bank (NDB), which provides loans for infrastructure projects. These institutions provide a platform for the BRICS to use their own currencies and reduce the influence of the dollar.

Energy trading: Another area where the BRICS are challenging the dominance of the dollar is energy trading. China, Russia and Brazil are major energy producers and consumers. If they conduct trade in their own currencies, this could reduce the need for dollar transactions in the oil and gas sector and weaken the dollar's position as the reserve currency in this area. Especially since some Arab oil and gas producing countries are already following the example of the BRICS countries and also restricting payments in US dollars.

It is important to note, however, that the challenges to the dollar's dominance posed by the rise of the BRICS countries will not be immediate and without obstacles. The dollar still has a strong position in the global economy and is widely used in international financial markets, also due to political dependencies. In addition, there are also internal challenges in the BRICS countries, such as structural problems, political uncertainties and different economic policies that could affect their ability to overtake the dollar.

The rise of the BRICS countries undoubtedly poses a challenge to the dollar's dominance. Their economic potential and their aspirations to strengthen their own currencies internationally could reduce the dollar's influence in various areas such as international payments, trade, reserve currencies and energy trading. It is important to note, however, that the dollar's dominance is not under immediate threat and the process of change will be slow and complex. The dollar remains the dominant reserve currency for now, but developments in the BRICS countries are an important factor to watch as they can influence the dynamics in the global financial system.

An important factor influencing the dominance of the US dollar is the role of global financial markets. The BRICS countries have recognized that an international financial infrastructure is needed to strengthen their own currencies and create an alternative to the US dollar. China in particular has taken steps to internationalize the yuan and strengthen China's role as a financial center. The country has developed the Shanghai Stock Exchange and the Shenzhen Stock Exchange into major stock exchanges and facilitated trading in Chinese bonds and derivatives. In addition, China has encouraged the establishment of clearing houses for trading in Chinese currencies in various countries. These measures aim to facilitate international trade in Chinese currencies and reduce dependence on the US dollar.

Russia has also taken steps to limit the influence of the dollar. The country has increased its gold reserves and diversified its international foreign exchange reserves. In addition, Russia has entered into bilateral currency swap agreements with various countries to facilitate trade in national currencies. This is intended to help strengthen the role of the ruble and reduce the influence of the US dollar.

Another aspect that affects the dominance of the US dollar is the use of alternative payment systems. The BRICS countries have realized that they need to reduce their dependence on SWIFT (Society for Worldwide Interbank

Financial Telecommunication), the US-based payment system that handles the majority of international banking transactions. China has already introduced the Cross-Border Interbank Payment System (CIPS) to facilitate cross-border payments in Chinese currencies and reduce dependence on SWIFT. Russia has announced similar plans to develop its own national payment system to strengthen its financial independence. These alternative payment systems are intended to help limit the influence of the US dollar and increase the sovereignty of the BRICS countries in financial matters.

In addition, the BRICS countries have also taken initiatives to establish their own regional development bank. In 2014, the Asian Infrastructure Investment Bank (AIIB) was launched, involving both China and other BRICS countries. The AIIB is intended to finance infrastructure projects in Asia and provide an alternative to the World Bank, which is dominated by Western countries. By creating such regional financial institutions, the BRICS countries aim to gain greater autonomy in developing and financing their own infrastructure projects.

It is important to note that the process of reducing the influence of the US dollar is long-term and complex. The US dollar has held a strong position as the world's reserve currency for many decades and is firmly entrenched in many areas of the global economy. The transition to a multipolar world order in which the influence of the US dollar is limited will require close cooperation and coordination among the BRICS countries and a steady development of their economic and financial systems.

It remains to be seen how the military and political leverage of the BRICS countries will evolve in relation to the supremacy of the US dollar. While the BRICS countries have made progress in strengthening their economic sovereignty and reducing the influence of the dollar, for now the US dollar remains the dominant reserve currency and the currency of choice for international trade. The BRICS countries face challenges such as integrating their national markets, strengthening their institutions and creating a stable economic environment to achieve their goals.

The BRICS countries have enormous economic potential and have grown into significant players in the global economy. Each country has its own strengths and challenges to overcome. Brazil benefits from its natural resources and agribusiness, Russia from its energy resources and industry, India from its large population and IT sector, China from its manufacturing capacity and technology sector, and South Africa from its diversity of industries and its role in Africa. However, the BRICS countries also have to deal with a number of challenges, such as inequality, corruption, political instability and environmental problems. Nevertheless, their rise in the global economy is remarkable and it will be exciting to see how their potentials continue to unfold in the future.

Potential for cooperation and synergies

Despite the potential challenges to the dollar's dominance, the rise of the BRICS also presents opportunities for cooperation and synergies. By combining their resources, markets and technological advances, the BRICS can work together to strengthen their economic development and consolidate their position in the global economy.

Trade and investment: By increasing trade and investment among themselves, the BRICS can deepen their economic cooperation. By reducing trade barriers, reducing tariffs and creating investment incentives, they can promote bilateral trade and benefit from each other. For example, Brazil could export its agricultural products to China while India imports Chinese electronic products. By exchanging goods and services, the BRICS can diversify their economies and reduce their dependence on other countries.

Infrastructure projects: The BRICS have the potential to implement joint infrastructure projects. This could facilitate trade and exchange between the countries and promote their regional integration. For example, building roads, railways and port facilities could improve logistics and make freight transport more efficient. The BRICS could also invest in renewable energy and initiate joint projects to develop clean energy.

Technology transfer: Each of the BRICS countries has specific know-how and technological advancements in different fields. By sharing knowledge and technologies, they can learn from each other and strengthen their innovation capacities. For example, China is a leader in 5G technology and could share its knowledge with the other

BRICS countries. India, on the other hand, is a major player in the IT sector and could share its expertise in this area.

Joint research and development: The BRICS countries could also invest in joint research and development projects. By collaborating in areas such as medicine, biotechnology, space and environmental sciences, they could find innovative solutions and strengthen their competitiveness. This could also help reduce dependence on technologies and innovations from other parts of the world.

Despite the potential challenges to dollar dominance, there are opportunities for cooperation and synergies for the BRICS countries. By expanding trade, joint infrastructure projects, technology transfer and joint research and development, they can strengthen their economic development and consolidate their position in the global economy. By combining their resources and competencies, the BRICS countries can reduce their dependence on other countries and advance their regional integration. It will be exciting to see how this cooperation will develop in the future and what impact it will have on the global economy.

The Bretton Woods System

The Bretton Woods System was an international monetary system developed during the Bretton Woods Conference in 1944 in New Hampshire, USA. The system's goal was to stabilize the global economy after World War II and promote trade, as well as to secure the financial and geopolitical dominance of the United States.

The Bretton Woods System was based on two main institutions: the International Monetary Fund (IMF) and the International Bank for Reconstruction and Development (IBRD), which are now part of the World Bank Group. The IMF was established to promote economic cooperation between countries and to provide financial support, while the IBRD provided loans for war-damaged reconstruction.

A central component of the Bretton Woods System was the fixed exchange rate peg of the US dollar to gold. The other participating countries agreed to peg their currencies to the US dollar. This made the dollar the reserve currency of the system. Currencies were backed by gold or the U.S. dollar, which provided a certain level of stability.

Another feature of the system was the setting of exchange rate limits. Participating countries were only allowed to let their currencies fluctuate within a certain percentage range around the set exchange rate. This was intended to prevent excessive exchange rate fluctuations and keep trading conditions stable.

The Bretton Woods system worked relatively well for some time, but it began to come under pressure in the 1960s. The U.S. had a large trade deficit and had to spend more and more dollars to meet its obligations to other countries. At the same time, it became more difficult to keep the promise that dollars could be exchanged for gold.

In 1971, then-U.S. President Richard Nixon decided to stop the convertibility of the dollar into gold and float the exchange rate. This led to the collapse of the Bretton Woods system. After that, flexible exchange rates developed, where currencies could be traded in a free market.

Despite its collapse, the Bretton Woods system had a major impact on the international economic order. It created institutions such as the IMF and the World Bank, which continue to play an important role in promoting economic cooperation. It also laid the foundation for the idea of economic stability through international cooperation, thus shaping the development of the global financial system.

Reasons for the collapse of the Bretton Woods system:

Trade imbalances: Over time, trade imbalances developed in many countries as some countries exported more than they imported while other countries did the opposite. These imbalances led to balance of payments imbalance and accumulation of foreign exchange reserves in some countries.

Speculation against the US dollar: Due to the convertibility of the US dollar into gold, some speculators started selling the dollar and buying gold instead. This led to pressure on the US gold reserves and weakened the link between the dollar and the gold standard.

Inflation and deflation: Some countries were forced to devalue their currencies to promote their exports and improve their trade balance. This led to inflationary pressures in some countries and deflationary pressures in others. However, the Bretton Woods system had no mechanisms to deal with such situations.

Inflexibility of exchange rates: The fixed exchange rates of the Bretton Woods system left little room for adjustment in response to economic shocks or changes in relative competitiveness. This led to tensions between countries and limited their ability to respond to economic problems.

De-pegging of the dollar: In 1971, the US government under President Richard Nixon decided to de-peg the US dollar into gold. This marked the end of the gold standard and weakened the foundation of the Bretton Woods system.

As a result of these factors, the mechanisms of the Bretton Woods system collapsed, leading to a transition to flexible exchange rates and a new international monetary system.

The Bretton Woods system made perfect sense in the post-World War II period, as the post-war global political situation required a new global financial architecture. The world economy was in ruins in the majority of countries after the war. At the same time, it secured the leading political position of the USA. It should not be forgotten that the United States faced what it considered a dangerous opponent - the communist countries led by the then USSR.

The system was based on the US dollar as the reserve currency, which was pegged to gold. Other currencies were pegged to the US dollar, resulting in fixed exchange rates. This created relative stability and predictability in the international financial and trade markets, which facilitated investment.

The Bretton Woods system also led to the creation of the International Monetary Fund (IMF) and the World Bank. These institutions were designed to help member countries with financial difficulties and support post-war reconstruction. They promoted economic cooperation.

The creation of an international financial system after World War II was crucial to promote economic reconstruction and stability in a time of uncertainty. The Bretton Woods system facilitated trade, promoted the growth of the global economy, and helped prevent further conflict.

However, the Bretton Woods system was not sustainable in the long term and came under pressure in the 1970s. It led to exchange rate instability and the abandonment of the gold standard of the US dollar. Nevertheless, the Bretton Woods system remains an important milestone in the development of the international financial system and helped to rebuild the world economy after World War II.

The role of the US-Dollar in the international financial system

The international financial system plays a crucial role in the global economy. It allows for trade between countries, the transfer of capital, and the granting of credit. One of the main currencies used in the international financial system is the U.S. dollar. The dollar has a long history as the dominant reserve currency and significantly influences financial markets worldwide.

To understand the role of the dollar in the international financial system, it is important to look back to the post-war period. After the end of World War II, the U.S. economy established itself as one of the strongest in the world, as the U.S. economy had survived the war largely unscathed. The U.S. was the largest creditor nation and held a significant amount of gold reserves. This led to the Bretton Woods agreement in 1944, which established the dollar as the anchor currency.

Under the Bretton Woods system, the dollar was pegged to gold and other currencies were pegged to the dollar. This fixation enabled stable exchange rates and encouraged trade between countries. The dollar became the world's main reserve currency and the US assumed responsibility for guaranteeing the dollar's value against gold.

However, challenges to the Bretton Woods system began in the 1960s. The US was putting more and more money into circulation to finance its military spending and social programs. At the same time, the US trade and current account deficits were increasing. Other countries began to have doubts about the dollar's value and demanded that dollars be convertible into gold.

In 1971, the US government could no longer keep up the pressure and decided to remove the dollar's convertibility into gold. This marked the end of the Bretton Woods system and an important turning point in the dollar's history. From then on, the dollar became a pure fiat currency* whose value was based on the confidence of the markets and the strength of the US economy.

**The term "FIAT currency" refers to a currency issued by a government or central bank as the official means of payment of a country. The term "FIAT" comes from Latin and means "let it be." In the context of currencies, this means that the value of a FIAT currency is not based on a physical asset such as gold or silver, but on people's trust in the authority that issues it.*

Essentially, the value of a FIAT currency is based on people's trust and acceptance that it can be used to purchase goods, services, and pay debts. The government or central bank regulates the money supply, controls the exchange rate, and conducts monetary policy actions to maintain the stability of the currency.

Because FIAT currencies are not backed by a fixed value such as gold, they can be susceptible to inflation or devaluation. Monetary policy, economic growth, demand and supply in the foreign exchange market, and geopolitical factors can affect the value of a FIAT currency.

Most currencies in the world are FIAT currencies, including the Euro, US dollar, Japanese yen, British pound, and many others.

(Source: Wikipedia)

After the collapse of the Bretton Woods system, the dollar began to further expand its role as the dominant reserve currency. Most countries in the world held large amounts of dollar reserves to stabilize their currencies and settle international transactions. The dollar became the primary currency for international trade of commodities such as oil.

The strength of the dollar in the international financial system also affects other countries. Since the dollar is the dominant reserve currency, many countries are forced to peg their currencies to the dollar to maintain stable exchange rates. This can create challenges, especially for countries with weak economies, as they have less control over their monetary policies.

Another aspect that shapes the role of the dollar in the international financial system is the fact that the US is the largest economy in the world. The dollar is seen as a safe haven, and many investors hold dollar assets to protect their capital. This gives the US some influence over global financial markets and allows it to advance its interests.

However, there is also criticism of the dollar's dominance in the international financial system. Some argue that the US may abuse its power to achieve its economic and political goals. In addition, dependence on a single currency, especially a fiat currency, and the associated exchange rate fluctuations pose a risk to the stability of the global financial system.

To mitigate these risks, some countries have tried to reduce the use of the dollar in international trade. They are concluding bilateral trade agreements that allow currencies to be exchanged directly without going through the dollar. In addition, alternative reserve currencies such as the euro and the Chinese yuan have become increasingly popular.

Despite these efforts, however, the dollar remains the dominant reserve currency for the time being and plays a crucial role in the international financial system. The USA is doing everything it can to secure its dominance in this regard. It is certainly using political and military means to do so. The USA sees itself as having a great responsibility to ensure the stability of the dollar and to maintain market confidence.

One area in which the dollar plays a particularly important role is international trade. Many countries use the dollar as their standard currency for trading goods and services. For example, if a company from Germany buys goods from China, these are often settled in dollars. This is because the dollar is a stable currency and is accepted worldwide. By using the dollar as a trading currency, companies can minimize currency risks and facilitate trade transactions. However, this is countered by the double exchange into the respective national currencies and the double costs for this.

Another role of the dollar in the international financial system is its use as a reserve currency. Many central banks hold a significant portion of their foreign exchange reserves in the form of dollars. This serves to support the stability of national currencies and provide a solid foundation for international payments. The fact that the dollar is widely used as a reserve currency also gives the U.S. a strong influence over the monetary policies of other countries.

The dollar is also the preferred currency for international loans and bonds. When a country takes out a loan or issues bonds, it is often denominated in dollars. This is partly because the dollar has been viewed as a stable currency to date, which increases investor confidence. In addition, the use of the dollar as a loan and bond instrument allows access to a wider pool of investors around the world.

Another aspect that shapes the role of the dollar in the international financial system is the fact that many international financial institutions are headquartered in the U.S. The World Bank, the International Monetary Fund (IMF), and other major institutions use the dollar as the primary currency for their activities. This underscores the importance of the dollar as the language of international finance and gives the US control over these institutions, which is viewed as critical by some actors who see it as compromising their economic and political freedom of choice.

In addition, the dollar has a strong position in foreign exchange markets. Foreign exchange trading, which involves buying and selling currencies, is an important part of the international financial system. The dollar is the most widely traded currency and accounts for a large share of daily foreign exchange trading volume. This is partly due to the liquidity of the dollar market and the widespread acceptance of the dollar.

However, there are also challenges and risks associated with the dollar's role in the international financial system. One of these is the potential volatility of the exchange rate. Since many countries peg their currencies to the dollar or hold large dollar reserves, changes in the dollar's exchange rate can have a significant impact on those countries. Sudden declines in the dollar's value could cause economic turmoil and affect confidence in the international financial system.

Another risk is that the US may abuse its economic or political power to advance its interests. Because the dollar plays a dominant role in the international financial system, the US may take sanctions or other measures to restrict access to dollar payments or transactions. This may pose a challenge for other countries and lead to tensions in international relations.

Despite these challenges, the dollar remains the dominant reserve currency for now and plays a central role in the international financial system. The US has a strong vested interest in maintaining the stability of the dollar and preserving market confidence. At the same time, there are efforts by other countries and international institutions to reduce dependence on the dollar and promote alternative currencies or mechanisms.

Overall, the role of the dollar in the international financial system is complex and has far-reaching implications for global economics and politics. The evolution of the international financial architecture will continue to be shaped by different actors and interests. It remains to be seen how this dynamic will evolve in the future and to what extent alternative currencies or approaches will gain in importance.

To ensure its dominance in the international financial system, the United States employs various strategies. One important method is to ensure that the dollar is viewed as an attractive currency for investment and transactions.

This is done by maintaining a stable economic environment, strong monetary policy, and ongoing regulation of the financial sector.

The U.S. central bank, the Federal Reserve, plays a central role in maintaining the strength of the dollar. Through its monetary policy, the Federal Reserve influences the value of the dollar and interest rates, which impacts the currency's attractiveness to investors. The Federal Reserve aims to promote price stability and appropriate economic development in order to increase confidence in the dollar.

Another method the United States uses to defend the dollar's dominance is to work closely with other countries and international institutions. The United States works closely with allies to promote the use of the dollar in international

The United States works closely with allies to promote the use of the dollar in international transactions and to establish trade agreements that secure the dollar as the preferred currency in the world. This is done, for example, through bilateral agreements or by supporting multilateral institutions such as the International Monetary Fund (IMF), which supports the use of the dollar in certain situations and countries.

Another approach is to maintain the liquidity of the dollar market. The dollar is traded widely around the world, and the U.S. strives to ensure that there is sufficient dollar liquidity to keep the international financial system running smoothly. This includes the Federal Reserve providing dollar loans and liquidity or working with other central banks to establish swap agreements that facilitate access to dollars.

Furthermore, the U.S. uses its political and economic power to promote the use of the dollar. It uses sanctions or other economic measures to control access to dollar payments or transactions and to enforce its geopolitical goals. This can force other countries to accept the dollar as a preferred currency to avoid economic disadvantages. Through these methods, the U.S. can maintain the influence of the dollar and assert its dominance in the international financial system.

In addition, the role of the U.S. dollar in international trade also plays a crucial role in defending its dominance. The dollar is used as a currency for global trade almost everywhere in the wor**ld, especially in the area of** commodities such as oil. The United States encourages the use of the dollar in international trade and works closely with major trading partners to use various methods to ensure that the dollar remains the preferred currency. By facilitating trade in dollars, the United States remains at the center of international trade and strengthens its position as a leading economic power.

US political influence is a significant factor in defending the dollar's dominance in the international financial system. The United States uses its political and diplomatic power to ensure that the dollar is viewed as the preferred currency and that other countries accept and use the dollar.

One tool the United States uses to enforce its political goals is economic sanctions. The United States can impose sanctions on countries or individuals who act against its political interests. Because the dollar is the dominant currency in the international financial system, sanctions that restrict access to dollar payments or transactions have a significant impact on the economies of the countries affected. This may result in these countries being forced to accept the dollar as their preferred currency to mitigate the impact of the sanctions.

In addition, the US uses its political influence to influence international institutions and promote the use of the dollar. Institutions such as the International Monetary Fund (IMF) and the World Bank, which are significantly influenced by the US, play an important role in shaping the global financial architecture. The US works to ensure that these institutions support and encourage the use of the dollar. This can be done, for example, by lending in dollars or using the dollar as the main currency for IMF programs.

Another factor affecting the US's political influence on the dollar's supremacy is its military presence and power. The US is heavily involved militarily around the world and has military bases in various parts of the world. This military presence allows the US to exert political pressure and enforce its interests.

The US's military power can help ensure the stability of the dollar. By acting as a global superpower, the US can control and secure what is happening in the markets, thus promoting the acceptance of the dollar as a reserve currency. The US's ability to protect its interests through military means gives its currency additional strength and influence.

It is important to note, however, that US political influence and military power also have controversial aspects. Some argue that the US can abuse its power to achieve its economic and political goals, which can lead to tensions and conflicts. In addition, military interventions and conflicts can have negative effects on the stability of the global financial system and affect market confidence.

Overall, US political influence, including its military power, is a key factor in defending the dollar's supremacy. Through political actions such as economic sanctions and diplomatic efforts, the US enforces its interests and promotes the use of the dollar as the preferred currency.

However, it is important to consider the impacts and risks of this political and military influence and to find other sustainable solutions to ensure the stability of the international financial system.

The Petrodollar System and the BRICS Countries

The petrodollar system and the BRICS countries represent two important elements of the global economic order. While the petrodollar system is closely linked to the US dollar and international oil trade, the BRICS countries represent an emerging group of so-called emerging economies.

The petrodollar system is an arrangement based on the close connection between the US dollar and global oil trade. It emerged in the 1970s after OPEC (Organization of Petroleum Exporting Countries) decided to set oil prices in US dollars. This meant that other countries were forced to invest their foreign exchange reserves in US dollars in order to be able to import oil.

The US has a strong interest in ensuring that oil imports continue to be paid for in US dollars.

By settling oil imports in US dollars, the demand for US dollars is increased. This strengthens the US dollar as the dominant reserve currency and promotes its international acceptance. This gives the US a unique advantage in the global financial architecture. By tying the oil trade to the US dollar, a high demand for the currency is created. Other countries that want to import oil must exchange their own currency for US dollars to facilitate the purchase of oil. This leads to increased demand for US dollars in the foreign exchange markets, which supports the value of the currency. At the same time, national currencies are weakened against the dollar.

By tying the oil trade to the US dollar, the US has some control over the global oil market. It can make political and economic decisions that affect the price of oil and thus the entire global economy. This gives the US geopolitical leverage and allows it to effectively defend its interests against independence movements.

By tying the oil trade to the US dollar, a high demand for the currency is created. This allows the US to print large amounts of US dollars and accumulate large amounts of debt, as other countries are forced to hold their foreign exchange reserves in US dollars. The US can use these dollars to finance its own spending and service its debt.

The origin of the petrodollar dates back to 1973, when OPEC, in response to the Yom Kippur War, decided to reduce oil production and cause oil prices to rise. At the same time, OPEC members agreed to sell oil exclusively in US dollars, thus establishing the US dollar as the dominant reserve currency.

The challenges and criticisms of the Petrodollar system:

Despite its advantages, the petrodollar system also comes with some challenges and criticisms. One problem is that the US is taking inflation risks through its excessive use of the privilege of printing dollars. In addition, other countries, especially oil-importing states, are dependent on the fluctuations of the US dollar, making their economies vulnerable. In addition, some countries have started to challenge the petrodollar by introducing alternative payment systems and currencies for oil trading.

The idea of BRICS first emerged in 2001, when then-Goldman Sachs chief economist Jim O'Neill described the group as an emerging economic power in a report. In 2006, the first formal meeting of BRICS leaders took place, and since then member countries have held regular summits to strengthen their cooperation.

In recent years, various initiatives have emerged aimed at challenging the U.S. dollar as the dominant reserve currency and means of payment in global trade. One example is the introduction of the Chinese yuan as an alternative trading currency. China has taken steps to promote the international use of the yuan and to enter into bilateral trade agreements that use the yuan as a means of payment instead of the U.S. dollar.

In addition, some countries, particularly those affected by U.S. sanctions, have begun to develop alternative payment systems to break away from dependence on the U.S. dollar. One example is Russia's SWIFT-like payment system, which aims to reduce the impact of US sanctions on the Russian financial sector.

Another factor that could challenge the petrodollar system is changes in the global energy market. In recent years, an energy transition has taken place, with renewable energy and alternative energy sources playing an increasingly important role. The decline in demand for fossil fuels, particularly oil, could cause the value of the petrodollar to decline, making the system less attractive.

There are countries that have significant oil reserves but are not part of the petrodollar system. One example is Iran, which has been unwilling to sell its oil in exchange for US dollars due to political tensions and sanctions. Such developments could weaken the role of the petrodollar and favor alternative payment mechanisms.

The geopolitical shifts in international relations could also impact the petrodollar system. One example is the rise of China as an economic and political power. China has increasingly sought to establish its currency and the yuan as an alternative reserve currency. If China succeeds, this could further reduce the influence of the US dollar and weaken the petrodollar system.

The BRICS countries, particularly China and Russia, have taken a clear stance against the dominance of the petrodollar and have increased their efforts to promote alternative payment mechanisms and currencies. This could lead to an increasing influence of the BRICS countries in the international financial sector and further challenge the petrodollar system.

Given the challenges and changes in the global financial system, it is difficult to accurately predict the future development of the petrodollar system. However, there are some possible developments that could emerge in the coming years.

Given the uncertainties and risks associated with the petrodollar system, many countries may diversify their foreign exchange reserves and hold alternative currencies. This would result in the US dollar losing importance as the dominant reserve currency and other currencies, such as the Chinese yuan, gaining influence.

Some regions may seek to develop their own regional payment systems to break away from dependence on the petrodollar. One example of this is the Eurasian Economic Union, which has made efforts to build its own payment system to facilitate trade between member countries and reduce dependence on the US dollar.

The continued development of cryptocurrencies could also play a role in challenging the petrodollar system. Some cryptocurrencies already provide alternative payment mechanisms and could play a larger role in international transactions in the future. This would reduce the need for a dominant reserve currency, such as the US dollar.

The petrodollar system is facing challenges and changes that could affect its long-term stability and importance. The rise of alternatives to the US dollar, changes in the global energy market, and geopolitical shifts are just some of the factors challenging the system. It remains to be seen how these developments will evolve and what impact they will have on the global economy. However, it is clear that the petrodollar faces significant challenges in a changing world order and adjustments may be necessary to maintain its role as a dominant reserve currency.

The Organization of Petroleum Exporting Countries (OPEC) plays a significant role in the dispute between the BRICS countries and the USA. OPEC consists of several member countries that together control a significant portion of global oil production. Their decisions and actions have a direct impact on the international oil market and thus also on the petrodollar system.

The OPEC countries have a significant influence on the global oil market because they together own a significant portion of the world's oil reserves and production. Through their decisions on production quotas and pricing, they can influence supply and demand on the oil market. This in turn affects oil prices, which play a crucial role in the petrodollar system. However, the OPEC countries are heavily dependent on the petrodollar because the majority of their oil exports are settled in US dollars. This means that they themselves have an interest in maintaining the stability and acceptance of the petrodollar.

The BRICS countries, especially China and Russia, have increasingly taken initiatives in recent years to reduce their dependence on the petrodollar system.

They have encouraged the development of alternative payment systems and the use of other currencies for oil trading. For example, China, which is one of the largest oil importers in the world, has entered into bilateral trade agreements in which the yuan is used as payment for oil.

If alternative payment systems and currencies gain importance in oil trading, this will weaken the position of the petrodollar and thus the stability of the petrodollar. This could create a dilemma for OPEC countries as they would have to trade off between maintaining their dependence on the petrodollar and adapting to alternative payment systems.

A potential conflict between the BRICS and the US regarding the petrodollar system and alternative payment systems would also have implications for the US. The petrodollar system has provided numerous benefits to the US, including strengthening the US dollar as a reserve currency and the ability to accumulate large amounts of debt. A challenge to this system could therefore affect the stability of the US dollar and massively weaken the economic strength of the US.

In addition, a decrease in the demand for US dollars in oil trading would reduce the attractiveness of the US dollar as an international reserve currency. This could lead to a redistribution of foreign exchange reserves and a shift in global financial flows in favor of other currencies.

The role of the OPEC countries in the dispute between the BRICS and the US related to the petrodollar system is of great importance. As significant players in the global oil market, the majority of OPEC countries have an interest in maintaining the stability of the petrodollar. At the same time, the BRICS countries, especially China and Russia, are increasingly looking for alternative payment systems and currencies to reduce their dependence on the petrodollar system. This could lead to an increasing challenge for the OPEC countries and the petrodollar system as a whole. The impact of this conflict on the USA would be significant and could lead to changes in the global financial architecture.

While the petrodollar system is striving to consolidate the US dollar as the reserve currency in global oil trading, the BRICS countries are striving for greater economic and political autonomy and the development of their own monetary system. The effects of these developments are diverse and range from geopolitical shifts to challenges to the established financial system. It remains to be seen how these issues will develop in the future and what impact they will have on the global economy.

The BRICS Countries as an alternative to the US-Dollar

The BRICS countries, consisting of Brazil, Russia, India, China and South Africa, have experienced a remarkable economic rise in recent decades. These emerging economies have increased their efforts to play a larger global role and to move away from dependence on the US dollar as the primary reserve currency. In this chapter, we will look at how the BRICS countries could develop an alternative to the dollar and what impact this would have on the international economy.

The global economy has long been dominated by the US dollar, which was considered the leading reserve currency and the primary means of payment for international transactions. This led to a heavy dependence on economic and monetary developments in the United States. The BRICS countries have recognized that this dependence poses a risk and that it is important to develop alternative mechanisms to protect their own interests.

A first step towards an alternative to the dollar was the establishment of the New Development Bank (NDB) by the BRICS in 2014. This multilateral development bank aims to finance infrastructure projects in member countries and promote cooperation in the areas of trade and investment. The NDB represents an alternative to existing institutions such as the World Bank and the International Monetary Fund, which are dominated by Western countries.

In addition, the BRICS have taken steps to strengthen their bilateral trade relations and encourage the use of national currencies in their transactions. A good example of this is the growing trade between China and Russia, which is increasingly being settled in yuan and rubles, rather than dollars. This reduces dependence on the dollar and strengthens the resilience of the BRICS to external economic shocks.

Another step towards an alternative to the dollar could be the creation of a common currency among the BRICS. Similar to the euro in the European Union, a common currency would facilitate trade and integration among member countries and reduce dependence on the dollar. However, this would be a complex process that would require close economic and political cooperation.

An important aspect of developing an alternative to the dollar is strengthening the BRICS as a unit and their cooperation in international forums such as the G20. By acting together and raising their voices in global economic affairs, the BRICS can better represent their interests and play a greater role in shaping the international financial architecture.

It is important to note, however, that developing an alternative to the dollar is not an easy task and may involve many challenges. The dollar has established itself as a stable and trusted reserve currency over many decades, and it will take time and efforts to create an alternative currency or mechanisms that can gain the trust of the international community.

It can be said that the BRICS are increasingly striving to develop an alternative to the dollar and reduce their dependence on the US currency. The establishment of the New Development Bank and the strengthening of bilateral trade relations are important steps in this direction.

However, it will take time and intensive cooperation to achieve these goals. The BRICS have the potential to play a larger global role and change the international financial architecture, but it remains to be seen how successful their efforts will be.

The BRICS have increased their efforts in recent years to develop an alternative to the US dollar as a primary reserve currency. In addition to establishing the New Development Bank and strengthening bilateral trade relations, they have taken other measures to reduce their dependence on the dollar.

An interesting step in this direction has been the introduction of currency swaps among the BRICS. These are agreements in which the central banks of the countries involved exchange their national currencies with each other to facilitate trade and investment. This reduces the need to use the dollar as an intermediate currency and strengthens financial cooperation within the BRICS.

In addition, the BRICS have also promoted the exchange of government bonds in national currencies. This allows the participating countries to issue their bonds in their own currencies and promotes the trading of debt instruments among themselves.

This strengthens the liquidity of national currencies and contributes to the diversification of reserve currencies.

Another approach that the BRICS countries are pursuing is to promote gold trading in their national currencies. Gold has traditionally played an important role as a store of value and a hedge against currency risks. By facilitating the trading of gold in their own currencies, the BRICS countries can further reduce their dependence on the dollar and strengthen their currencies as reserve currencies.

In addition to these concrete measures to diversify their reserve currencies, the BRICS countries have also made political and diplomatic efforts to represent their interests at the international level. They have increased their cooperation in various areas such as trade, investment, technology, education and culture. Through this close cooperation, the BRICS countries not only strengthen their bilateral trust with each other, but also their position in international negotiations and can jointly advocate for reform of the global financial architecture.

In addition, the BRICS countries must also consider possible challenges and risks that may be associated with a move away from the dollar. A transition that is too rapid or uncoordinated could lead to market uncertainty and destabilising effects. It is therefore important that the BRICS countries plan their strategies carefully and implement them in close cooperation.

One thing is certain, however: by promoting the use of their national currencies in trade, developing financial institutions such as the New Development Bank and deepening their political and diplomatic cooperation, the BRICS countries can lay a solid foundation for an alternative reserve currency.

It remains to be seen how successful these efforts will ultimately be. The global financial architecture is complex and strongly influenced by historical and political factors. It requires continuous adaptation and development of strategies to ensure long-term success. Political disputes must be overcome and pushed aside.

In conclusion, it can be said that the BRICS countries are on the way to developing an alternative to the dollar. Through a combination of concrete measures to diversify their reserve currencies and increased cooperation at the political and diplomatic level, they can strengthen their independence from the dollar and play a greater role in the global financial architecture. It remains exciting to see how these developments unfold in the coming years.

The BRICS countries have initiated several major joint projects in the past:

New Development Bank (NDB): The BRICS countries jointly launched the NDB to finance infrastructure projects in the member countries. The bank has already financed various projects, including road construction, energy production and telecommunications.

Space cooperation: The BRICS countries have shown interest in cooperation in the field of space. Discussions have been held on the exchange of technologies and know-how to carry out joint space missions.

Energy projects: The BRICS countries have pushed forward joint projects in the field of renewable energies. These include the expansion of solar energy and research into bioenergy.

Research and education cooperation: The BRICS countries have launched various programs to promote cooperation in the fields of education and research. The exchange of students, scientists and experts between the countries is encouraged in order to learn from each other and initiate joint research projects.

The New Silk Road: The New Silk Road, also known as the Belt and Road Initiative (BRI), is a planned development project of the Chinese government. It is an ambitious infrastructure program that aims to create links between Asia, Europe, the Middle East, Africa and other regions.

The concept of the New Silk Road is based on the historic Silk Road, a network of trade routes that enabled the exchange of goods, ideas and cultures between East and West centuries ago. With the New Silk Road, China aims to create similar economic and cultural links by funding and developing modern infrastructure projects.

The project includes the construction of roads, railways, ports, airports and energy infrastructure to promote trade and economic integration between the countries involved. It also aims to support economic development in poorer countries and promote cooperation in areas such as finance, education and tourism.

These projects demonstrate the BRICS countries' ambition to strengthen their cooperation in various fields and address common challenges. However, it is important to note that the implementation of these projects may be at different stages of development and is influenced by political, economic and other factors.

The growing influence of the BRICS on developing countries as competitors to the US dollar is an interesting aspect to be examined. In recent years, the BRICS have increased their efforts to bring their own currencies into trade and financing of projects in developing countries. This has the effect of seriously competing with the US dollar as the dominant reserve currency and means of payment.

Another important reason for the growing influence of the BRICS on developing countries is their economic strength and increasing role as investors in these regions. Brazil, Russia, India, China and South Africa have significant foreign exchange reserves and have strong positions in areas such as infrastructure, energy, mining and agriculture. They are able to make large investments in development projects and offer financing options that do not necessarily require the US dollar.

An example of the growing influence of the BRICS on developing countries is China's role as a major lender and investor in Africa.

China has invested significant resources in the development of infrastructure projects in African countries in recent years. These investments often take the form of loans and financing provided in Chinese currency, the yuan. This reduces African countries' dependence on the US dollar and creates increased demand for the yuan as a means of payment and reserve currency.

Similar developments can be seen in other parts of the world. Russia, Brazil, India and South Africa have also begun to expand their investments in developing countries using their own currencies. This allows developing countries to reduce their dependence on the US dollar and hold a greater variety of reserve currencies.

Another factor that increases the influence of the BRICS countries on developing countries is their role as trading partners. By expanding trade between the BRICS countries and developing countries, the need for the US dollar as an intermediary currency is reduced. Instead, direct trade transactions are conducted in the national currencies of the countries involved. This facilitates trade and lowers transaction costs for developing countries.

It is important to note that the growing influence of the BRICS countries on developing countries does not necessarily mean that the US dollar will be completely displaced. The dollar continues to be a dominant reserve currency and an important means of payment on a global level. However, the BRICS countries have brought some diversity and flexibility to the international financial system with their efforts to introduce their own currencies as alternatives.

Reasons for developing countries to turn their backs on the US-Dollar

The US has often put its own economic interests above those of developing countries in the past. For example, resources such as oil, minerals and agricultural products from developing countries were exported at low prices while at the same time expensive imported products were sold to these countries. This led to an unequal trade balance and exploitation of developing countries.

The US political interference in the internal affairs of developing countries by overthrowing or supporting governments to further its own political interests often led to instability and conflict in these countries.

Developing countries were often lured with large loans to finance their infrastructure projects. However, these loans sometimes came with high interest rates and led to huge indebtedness in developing countries, making them dependent on the US and having difficulty repaying their debts.

Many US companies have used environmentally harmful practices in some developing countries to cut costs and maximize profits. This has led to air, water and soil pollution, which in turn has affected public health and environmental sustainability.

The dominance of American culture and media has led to the undermining of local cultures in some developing countries. Traditional values and practices have been replaced by imported Western ideas and consumer goods, leading to cultural homogenization.

These are just a few examples of the negative influence of the US on developing countries. There have certainly been positive examples of cooperation and support, but the aspects mentioned here illustrate the negative effects that have occurred in the past.

However, the growing competition to the US dollar from the BRICS countries offers advantages to developing countries. They now have more options when it comes to diversifying their reserve currencies and reducing their dependence on a single currency. This can improve their resilience to external shocks and changes in the global economy.

In addition, as competitors to the US dollar, the BRICS countries can also help reduce the cost of international transactions. If more transactions are made in national currencies, developing countries can potentially save costs associated with converting to and from the US dollar. This, in turn, can further strengthen trade and economic cooperation between the BRICS countries and developing countries.

Overall, the growing influence of the BRICS countries on developing countries as competitors to the US dollar is a remarkable phenomenon. The BRICS countries have used their economic strength to bring their own currencies into trade and financing projects in developing countries. In doing so, they have created an alternative to the dollar and provided developing countries with more options. It will be interesting to see how this trend evolves in the coming years and what impact it will have on the global financial architecture. It remains to be seen how the BRICS countries will deal with developing countries. It should not be forgotten that economic and political aspects are also important for them.

The influence of the BRICS countries as competitors to the US dollar on developing countries can be illustrated using a few concrete examples. I will discuss some notable cases below:

China has played a significant role in supporting economic development in African countries in recent years. Through extensive investments in infrastructure projects such as roads, railways, ports and energy plants, China has gained considerable influence on economic development in Africa. These investments are often financed in Chinese currency, the yuan, which helps to reduce dependence on the US dollar and strengthen the influence of the BRICS countries.

Russia has expanded its economic relations with Latin America and has become a major trading partner and investor in the region. In countries such as Venezuela and Cuba in particular, Russia has made investments in the energy and raw materials sectors. These investments are often made in Russian currency, the ruble, and offer Latin American countries an alternative to the US dollar.

India has increased its economic cooperation with South Asian countries such as Nepal, Sri Lanka and Bangladesh. In doing so, India has promoted the use of its own currency, the Indian rupee. Increasing trade in regional currencies reduces the need for the US dollar as an intermediate currency and strengthens the influence of the BRICS countries in developing countries.

Brazil has developed close economic cooperation with Angola in Africa. Brazilian companies are active in the energy, agriculture, infrastructure and banking sectors in Angola. Investments are often made in Brazilian currency, the real, which helps reduce dependence on the US dollar and strengthens the influence of the BRICS countries in the region.

These examples illustrate how the BRICS countries influence developing countries through their economic strength and the use of their own currencies in different regions of the world. By establishing trade and investment relationships that do not necessarily require the US dollar, they offer developing countries an alternative and expand their economic opportunities. This helps to reduce dependence on the US dollar and strengthen the BRICS countries' influence as competitors to the dollar.

It is important to note that these examples are just a few of a multitude of cases and that the BRICS countries' influence over developing countries continues to evolve. The BRICS countries continue their efforts to identify and implement new ways to strengthen their influence. However, the examples mentioned clearly illustrate the increaseing role of the BRICS countries as competitors to the US dollar in developing countries.

The motivation of the BRICS Countries

One of the most important issues facing the BRICS is the search for an alternative to the US dollar as the dominant world reserve currency. In this chapter, we will examine why the BRICS are seeking such an alternative, what opportunities they have already developed, and what potential impact this could have on the global economy.

The previous dominance of the US dollar brings both advantages and challenges. On the one hand, the US dollar, as a stable currency, enjoys the trust of investors and facilitates global trade. On the other hand, the BRICS and other emerging economies are heavily dependent on US dollar dominance, which can make their economies vulnerable to external shocks.

The BRICS have various motivations for seeking a counterweight to the increasingly uncertain US dollar. One of the main reasons is to reduce dependence on a single currency, especially given the political and economic uncertainties in the US. In addition, the BRICS want to strengthen their economic sovereignty and maintain control over their own currencies and financial markets. They see this as a crucial step to promote regional and global growth.

The BRICS countries have already taken various measures to develop alternative currencies and financial instruments. One example of this is the establishment of the New Development Bank (NDB) by the BRICS countries in 2014. The NDB is intended to serve as a financial institution and finance infrastructure projects in the BRICS countries. By creating this bank, the BRICS countries aim to reduce their dependence on established financial institutions such as the World Bank and the International Monetary Fund.

In addition, the BRICS countries have also strengthened their bilateral trade relations and entered into trade agreements in their national currencies. This allows them to bypass the US dollar in their trade relations and promote the use of their own currencies. This move aims to weaken the role of the US dollar as the dominant trading currency.

The efforts of the BRICS countries to create an alternative to the US dollar could have far-reaching effects on the global economy. Reducing dependence on the US dollar could lead to greater economic diversity and increase resilience to external shocks. At the same time, it could weaken the US dollar as the dominant reserve currency and change the international financial system.

It is important to note, however, that creating an alternative to the US dollar is a complex task and involves many challenges. The BRICS countries would need to build confidence in their own currency, develop their financial markets and gain international acceptance. They would also need to ensure close cooperation and coordination among themselves to create a coherent and effective alternative.

To illustrate the impact of the BRICS countries on dollar displacement and the development of alternatives, let us look at a concrete example. Let us assume that China and Russia decide to launch a joint initiative to bypass the US dollar in bilateral trade and use their own currencies.

China and Russia have strengthened their economic and political relations in recent years and are looking for ways to further expand their cooperation. Given the dominance of the US dollar in international markets, they have decided to explore alternative ways of conducting bilateral trade.

China and Russia agree to create a common currency mechanism that would allow trade between both countries in their national currencies. This mechanism would make it easier for companies to conduct business without having to go through the US dollar.

To facilitate the exchange and settlement of transactions in national currencies, China and Russia decide to create a special trading platform. This platform would allow companies to offer their products and services and trade in national currencies without the need to use the US dollar as an intermediary currency.

Given the success of the bilateral initiative between China and Russia, the other BRICS countries decide to join the initiative and create alternative trading mechanisms. Brazil, India and South Africa show great interest in the possibility of integrating their currencies more closely into international trade and reducing their dependence on the US dollar.

The BRICS countries recognize that they can not only strengthen their own trade relationships but also offer other countries alternatives to the US dollar. They are developing programs and initiatives to help other emerging and developing countries bypass the US dollar and trade in their national currencies.

The BRICS countries are offering financing opportunities, technical assistance and training to encourage the establishment of alternative trading mechanisms and the development of local currencies. This approach aims to strengthen the sovereignty and economic independence of the countries involved while challenging the role of the US dollar as the dominant world reserve currency.

The BRICS initiative to displace the dollar and offer alternatives would undoubtedly have an impact on the US dollar and the global economy. A reduction in demand for the dollar for international trade could lead to a devaluation of the currency and weaken the US position as a global financial power.

At the same time, the creation of alternatives would lead to a greater variety of reserve currencies and reduce dependence on a single currency. This could strengthen the resilience of the international financial system and give emerging economies a greater voice and influence in global financial issues.

The BRICS countries have the potential to create a significant alternative to the US dollar as the dominant world reserve currency. By developing bilateral trade mechanisms, common currency platforms and providing alternatives to other countries, they can challenge the role of the dollar and strengthen their own economic sovereignty.

It is important to note, however, that displacing the dollar and creating alternatives is a complex and long-term task. The BRICS countries would need to promote close cooperation, coordination and investment to achieve their goals. The impact on the global economy is difficult to predict and could depend on various factors. Nevertheless, the BRICS initiative shows that they are willing to explore new avenues and seek greater diversity in the international financial architecture.

The BRICS countries have a strong interest in creating an alternative to the US dollar as the dominant world reserve currency. By developing alternative currencies, financial instruments and trade agreements, they are trying to strengthen their economic sovereignty and reduce the influence of the US dollar in the world. The potential impact of such a development on the global economy is significant and it remains to be seen how the situation will evolve. The BRICS countries will continue to work to strengthen their position in the global economy and promote a greater diversity of international currencies.

Trade between the BRICS countries without the US dollar as an intermediate currency is of great importance and could have far-reaching effects on the countries involved and the global economy. By bypassing the dollar and trading in their national currencies, the BRICS countries are striving for greater economic sovereignty and independence.

Trading in national currencies allows the BRICS countries to reduce exchange rate risks. When the US dollar is used as an intermediate currency, the countries involved are vulnerable to fluctuations in the dollar exchange rate. By trading directly in their own currencies, the BRICS countries can minimize these risks and make their economic relations more stable.

Trading without the dollar can help improve the trade balance of the BRICS countries. By trading directly in their national currencies, they can increase their exports and better control their imports. This can help reduce trade imbalances and strengthen the competitiveness of the BRICS countries.

Trading without the dollar offers the BRICS countries the opportunity to strengthen and develop their own financial markets. By using their currencies for international trade, they create greater demand for their national currencies and promote liquidity in their financial markets. This can help improve their financial infrastructure and support the development of their local capital markets.

Trading without the dollar strengthens regional integration among the BRICS countries. By conducting their trade relations in their own currencies, they promote the exchange of goods, services and investments within the region. This can drive economic cooperation and integration among the BRICS countries and strengthen their position in the global economy.

Trading without the dollar thus poses a challenge to the dominance of the US dollar as the world reserve currency. By creating alternative trading mechanisms and bypassing the dollar, the BRICS countries reduce demand for the US currency and promote a greater variety of reserve currencies. This can diversify the international financial system and reduce dependence on a single currency.

Dollar-free trade between the BRICS and other countries could result in significant economic and political losses for the United States. Since the U.S. dollar has served as the dominant world reserve currency to date, a reduction in demand for the dollar and the use of alternative currencies would weaken the U.S.'s influence in the global economy and politics.

Dollar-free trade would lead to a decrease in demand for the U.S. dollar. If the BRICS and other countries use alternative currencies for international trade, the need for dollars as an intermediary and reserve currency would decrease. This could lead to a decline in the value of the dollar, which could affect the purchasing power of the U.S. currency and increase inflation in the U.S.

The dollar's dominance in the global economy would be challenged by dollar-free trade. If alternative currencies gain prominence and more countries bypass the dollar, this could lead to a shift in global reserve currencies. Less dependence on the dollar would see the U.S. in a weaker position in international financial matters and in enforcing economic sanctions, which could affect its political ability to act.

Trading without the US dollar could lead to a decline in US exports. If the BRICS and other countries settle their trade relations in their own currencies, American exporters could face additional hurdles as their goods and services are no longer directly invoiced in dollars. This could reduce the competitiveness of US exports and lead to a decline in exports, which could have a negative impact on the US economy.

Dollar-free trade would also lead to a weakening of US financial markets. With fewer trade transactions settled in dollars, this would lead to a decline in liquidity and trading volume in US financial markets. This would in turn lead to a loss of attractiveness for international investors and a decline in the influence of the US as a financial center.

Trading without the dollar as an intermediate currency would also weaken the US's political influence in the world.

Using alternative currencies and bypassing the dollar would limit the US's ability to exert political and economic leverage. This could affect its ability to assert its interests and influence international alliances.

A decrease in demand for the dollar, a loss of dollar dominance, a decline in US exports, a weakening of US financial markets and a loss of influence in world politics would be possible consequences. It remains to be seen how the situation between the two financial systems will develop and how the US will respond to these changes to protect its position in the global economy.

The cooperation of the BRICS Countries in the financial sector

The BRICS countries have undergone remarkable development in recent years. In addition to their economic importance, they have also assumed an increasingly important role in the financial sector. The cooperation between these emerging economies not only affects their own countries but also the global financial landscape. In this chapter, we will look in detail at the cooperation of the BRICS countries in the financial field, examining their goals, the milestones they have achieved and the challenges they face in the future.

To fully understand the development of BRICS cooperation in the financial field, it is important to take a look at the founding of this influential association. The idea of close cooperation between Brazil, Russia, India, China and South Africa was first formulated in 2001, when the four countries (excluding South Africa at the time) decided in an informal meeting to join forces to promote their economic development and strengthen their voice in international affairs.

In 2006, South Africa was admitted to the group and the BRICS countries began to meet regularly and further specify their goals. In the financial field in particular, they recognized the potential and need for joint cooperation and decided to take initiatives to strengthen their financial relations and promote their economic stability.

The BRICS countries have formulated clear objectives for their cooperation in the financial field. One of their main concerns is to reduce dependence on Western financial institutions and to gain greater control over their own financial systems. They wanted to position their currencies more internationally and promote trade among themselves in national currencies.

In addition, the cooperation also aims to create a fairer global financial architecture. The BRICS countries believe that the existing international financial institutions do not sufficiently represent the interests of emerging economies and that reform is urgently needed.

Another objective of the cooperation is to improve financial integration among the BRICS countries in order to promote regional economic development and create synergies. By sharing information, best practices and technological know-how, members can learn from each other and further develop their respective financial systems.

Since its establishment, the BRICS countries have already made significant progress in their financial cooperation. A key aspect is the establishment of the New Development Bank (NDB), formerly known as the BRICS Development Bank. This multilateral development bank was established in 2014 to finance infrastructure projects in the BRICS countries and thus support their economic development.

The creation of the NDB was a milestone for the BRICS countries as they now have their own financial institution, which gives them more autonomy and room for maneuver. The bank has already financed a number of projects, including the development of ports, roads and energy infrastructure in various BRICS countries. By supporting these projects, the NDB contributes to job creation, economic development and the promotion of trade within the BRICS countries.

Another important achievement of the cooperation is the establishment of a BRICS Monetary Fund. This fund aims to improve the currency stability and liquidity of the BRICS countries and to insulate them against external financial crises. The creation of this fund will allow member countries to draw on additional financial resources when needed, thereby protecting their currencies and stabilizing their financial systems.

Although the BRICS countries' financial cooperation has made considerable progress, they also face challenges that need to be addressed. One of the biggest challenges is the different economic and political orientations of the member countries. Each country has its own national interests and priorities, which can sometimes lead to tensions and disagreements. The BRICS countries must therefore find ways to maintain their cooperation despite these differences and pursue common goals.

Another challenge is the increasing competition between the BRICS countries themselves. Since they are all emerging economies, they compete directly with each other in some areas, be it trade, investment or the search for new markets. The BRICS countries must therefore shape their cooperation in a way that takes into account the individual interests of each country while promoting synergies and joint growth.

In the future, it will also be important to expand the BRICS countries' cooperation in the financial field to other areas. The digital economy, finance and sustainable finance are just some of the areas in which the BRICS countries can intensify their cooperation. Promoting innovation and technological progress will also be of great importance to ensure the economic success and competitiveness of the BRICS countries in the long term.

A promising approach to address these challenges and further deepen the BRICS countries' cooperation in the financial field is to expand the role of the BRICS Bank (NDB). The bank can serve as a platform to share expertise and resources in various fields, including the financial sector. By sharing best practices, expertise and technological know-how, the BRICS countries can learn from each other and further develop their respective financial systems.

Another promising step could be the establishment of a common digital currency of the BRICS countries. Given the rapid development of digital payment systems and cryptocurrencies, a digital currency of the BRICS countries could further promote their economic integration and facilitate trade between them. Such a currency would enable the BRICS countries to reduce their dependence on other international currencies.

In addition to strengthening bilateral relations, the BRICS countries should also intensify their efforts to reform the global financial architecture. They should actively work to ensure that their interests and concerns are adequately represented in international financial institutions. By increasing their participation and influence, the BRICS countries can help create a fairer and more balanced world economic order.

To further advance BRICS financial cooperation, it is important to promote dialogue and exchange between member countries. Regular summits and high-level meetings will be used to strengthen strategic partnerships, overcome political obstacles and identify new opportunities for cooperation. In addition, BRICS countries will intensify their cooperation with other emerging economies and create synergies to further strengthen their voice in international financial policy.

Another focus is on strengthening financial education and promoting financial professionals. By investing in the training and qualification of experts, BRICS countries ensure that they have the necessary expertise to develop and strengthen their financial systems. This will also help to further deepen financial cooperation and find innovative solutions to common challenges.

In conclusion, BRICS financial cooperation is a promising development that is of great importance both for member countries and for the global financial landscape. By expanding their cooperation, the BRICS countries promote their economic stability, strengthen their financial sovereignty and promote a fairer world economic order. It is important that the BRICS countries continue their efforts to deepen their cooperation, address challenges and find new ways to achieve their common goals. Only through close and constructive cooperation will the BRICS countries realize their potential and become a force that has a lasting impact on the global financial world.

The founding of the BRICS countries was based on a number of causes that made their cooperation seem necessary and meaningful in the global context.

One of the main reasons for the founding of the BRICS countries was, among others, the restrictive sanctions policy of the US financial world. In addition, the opportunity that lies in the considerable economic potential that exists in these emerging economies. Brazil, Russia, India, China and South Africa are countries with large populations, considerable natural resources and a growing demand for goods and services.

They have a solid industrial base, high production potential and a growing middle class that can make a significant contribution to global consumption. Given these factors, the countries recognised that closer cooperation in terms of trade, investment and economic integration offered great opportunities for growth and development.

The BRICS also formed their cooperation to strengthen their negotiating position in international affairs. Individually, the BRICS were already important players on the global stage, but by forming a solid unit, they were able to strengthen their voice in international institutions and forums such as the United Nations, the World Trade Organization and the International Monetary Fund. Together, they were able to better articulate their interests and act on an equal footing with established economic powers. Through their cooperation, the BRICS aimed to achieve a multipolar world order based on a fair distribution of power and influence.

The BRICS were also motivated by the need to reform the global financial architecture. After the global financial crisis of 2008, they realized that the existing international financial institutions, particularly the International Monetary Fund (IMF) and the World Bank, needed reforms to better reflect the interests of emerging economies. The BRICS countries felt that the distribution of votes and voting rights in these institutions was not adequate and that more equitable representation was needed. By working together, they were able to create a common platform to articulate these concerns and initiate reforms in the existing financial institutions.

The BRICS countries often have similar political goals and share certain views on global issues such as terrorism and multilateral diplomacy. By working together, they were able to better coordinate their political positions and support each other in international discussions and negotiations. The BRICS countries strive for a multipolar world order in which several powers and regions play a significant role and decisions are made jointly. This cooperation helps strengthen the sovereignty and independence of the BRICS countries and promotes an equal relationship between the various actors in the world.

In summary, the establishment of the BRICS countries was based on several causes. The economic potential and emerging markets of the BRICS countries, the strengthening of their negotiating position in global affairs, the need to reform the global financial architecture and the coordination of policy positions were decisive factors. The cooperation of the BRICS countries provides a platform for common interests, cooperation and the exchange of best practices to advance the growth and development of their economies and strengthen their voice in the international arena.

The BRICS countries have assumed an important role as a counterweight to US big capital. This role is based on various aspects, which are explained in detail below.

The BRICS countries have a wide range of economic activities and a diversity of resources, which allows them to be more independent of external influences. Unlike many developed economies that are heavily dependent on the financial sector and the service industry, the BRICS countries have a strong industrial base, rich natural resources and growing agricultural production. This diversity allows the BRICS countries to maintain a high degree of autonomy and be less vulnerable to external economic shocks. This allows them to achieve a certain degree of independence from US big capital and protect their own economic interests.

The BRICS countries have successfully established their own financial institutions, such as the New Development Bank (NDB) and the BRICS Monetary Fund. These institutions serve to strengthen their financial sovereignty and reduce their dependence on traditional Western financial institutions. By mobilizing their own financial resources and investing in infrastructure projects, trade facilitation and economic cooperation, the BRICS countries can advance their economic development and pursue their interests independently of the dominant players of US big capital.

Another important aspect is the promotion of trade between the BRICS countries in national currencies. Traditionally, trade between the countries was mainly conducted in US dollars, which led to dependence on the US financial system. By increasing the use of national currencies for trade between them, the BRICS countries can reduce their dependence on the US dollar and strengthen their own currencies. This helps to relativise the role of US big capital and to reduce the influence of the BRICS states.

This helps to relativize the role of US big capital and strengthen the influence of the BRICS countries in the global economy.

The BRICS countries have also taken measures to promote their economic sovereignty. This includes strengthening their industrial base, promoting research and development, developing their own technologies and diversifying their economies. Through these measures, the BRICS countries can reduce their dependence on foreign investment and technology and protect their own economic interests. This represents a counterweight to US big capital, which often tries to impose its economic interests in other countries.

The BRICS countries also cooperate at the political level to represent their common interests and act as a counterweight to US big capital. By working together, they can coordinate political positions, pursue common goals and strengthen their voice in international forums such as the United Nations and the G20 summit. By acting together, the BRICS countries can better articulate their interests and develop alternative visions for the global economic order that are not exclusively shaped by the interests of US big business.

In summary, the BRICS countries play an important role as a counterweight to US big capital. Through their economic diversity, the development of their own financial institutions, the promotion of trade in national currencies, the strengthening of economic sovereignty and political cooperation, the BRICS countries are able to pursue their interests independently of the dominant forces of US big capital. This contributes to a multipolar world order in which different actors can act on an equal footing and a greater variety of economic models and development paths is possible.

At the same time, however, it also creates new and increasing tensions in political and financial terms. The USA will not give up its supremacy without a fight and will use all available means to maintain its current position.

The impact of the BRICS Countries on the global economy

The BRICS countries have had a significant impact on the global economy over the past few decades. As emerging economic powers, they have strengthened their position on the global stage and recorded impressive growth rates. In this chapter, we will take a closer look at the impact of the BRICS countries on the global economy and analyze the various areas in which they have a significant influence.

The BRICS countries have experienced remarkable economic growth over the past few years. Their extensive natural resources, emerging markets and demographic advantages have provided them with a solid foundation for their economic development. China in particular, as the world's second largest economy, has a huge influence on the global economy. China's high growth rate has led to it becoming the workshop of the world, producing a significant share of global goods and services.

India has also established itself as an emerging economic power. With a growing middle class and a thriving IT industry, the country has become a major player in global trade and services such as information technology, outsourcing and telecommunications.

Brazil, known for its agricultural resources and thriving extractive industries, also has a significant impact on the global economy. The country is one of the largest producers of agricultural products such as soy, coffee and beef, and its commodity exports help stabilize global markets.

Russia, with its rich energy resources and highly developed defense industry, also has a significant impact on the global economy. The country is one of the largest producers and exporters of natural gas and plays a major role in the global energy market. In addition, Russia is one of the largest arms exporters in the world, which contributes to a significant impact on geopolitical dynamics.

South Africa, although economically smaller than the other BRICS countries, plays a major role on the African continent and also impacts the global economy. The country is rich in natural resources such as gold, platinum and diamonds and has a well-developed financial services industry.

The BRICS countries have also influenced global trade and investment. Through their rapidly growing domestic markets, they have become important trading partners for other countries. China, in particular, plays a prominent role in global trade. The country has established extensive trade relations with a wide range of countries and is both a major importer and exporter of goods and services. Through its growing middle class, China has also strengthened the consumer sector and influenced global consumption.

India has also expanded its trade relations and become a major player in global trade. The country exports a wide range of goods, including pharmaceutical products, IT services and textiles. In addition, India has attracted an increasing number of foreign direct investments, particularly in the information technology, automotive and service sectors.

Brazil has played an important role as a supplier of agricultural products and raw materials. The country exports a large amount of soybeans, coffee, sugar and meat products and has a strong presence in the global agricultural market. In addition, Brazil has attracted an increasing number of foreign investments, particularly in the energy, mining and infrastructure sectors.

Russia is a major exporter of oil, natural gas and other raw materials. The country has considerable influence on global energy markets and maintains close trade relations with various countries, especially in Europe and Asia. In addition, Russia also has a significant export market in the fields of armaments, engineering and technology.

South Africa has developed as a gateway to African markets and is an important trading partner for other African countries as well as for international investors. The country exports minerals, agricultural products and automotive components and has a well-established financial services industry that attracts investment.

The BRICS countries have also influenced the global financial system and international governance. They have created their own institution, the so-called "New Development Bank", which acts as an alternative to the World Bank and the International Monetary Fund (IMF). This bank aims to finance infrastructure projects in the BRICS countries and other developing countries and thus strengthen economic cooperation.

The BRICS also have a voice in international forums such as the G20, where they advocate for a fairer global economic order and greater participation of emerging economies. They have increased efforts to reduce the influence of developed countries in international governance and promote their own interests.

In addition, the BRICS have strengthened their bilateral trade and monetary relations. One example of this is the efforts by China and Russia to settle trade in their national currencies instead of using the US dollar. These efforts aim to reduce dependence on the US dollar as the world reserve currency and to strengthen the financial sovereignty of the BRICS.

The BRICS also have a significant influence on the global economy in terms of technological innovation and digital transformation. China in particular has emerged as a global technology leader. The country has made massive investments in areas such as artificial intelligence, robotics, e-commerce and mobile payment systems. Chinese companies such as Alibaba, Tencent and Huawei are world leaders in their respective industries and have revolutionized the way business is done.

India has also built on its strengths in the technology sector. The country is a major hub for software development, IT services and start-ups. Indian companies have developed innovative solutions in fintech, e-governance and healthcare and are contributing to digital transformation.

Brazil has excelled in the field of renewable energy. The country is one of the largest producers of bioethanol and has made significant progress in the development of solar and wind power in recent years. Brazilian companies also have a strong presence in telecommunications and software development.

Russia has shown its expertise in areas such as space, nuclear energy and defense technology. The country has made significant progress in space exploration and plays a major role in international space missions. Russian companies are also leaders in the nuclear energy industry and export their technologies to various countries.

South Africa has built on its strengths in information technology and telecommunications. The country has made significant progress in providing broadband internet and mobile services and has become a major hub for technology start-ups in Africa.

Despite their impressive growth and influence on the global economy, the BRICS also face a number of challenges. These include social inequality, environmental issues, political instability and economic volatility. Each country has its own specific challenges that must be addressed to achieve long-term sustainable growth.

However, the BRICS have significant potential to further strengthen their impact on the global economy. Through increased cooperation, trade facilitation and investment in education and infrastructure, they can increase their competitiveness and create new opportunities. In particular, promoting innovation, expanding the education system and creating a business-friendly environment are crucial to supporting the long-term growth of the BRICS.

In addition, the BRICS are increasingly taking a more active role in shaping global governance. By continuing to advocate for a fairer and more inclusive international economic order, they can increase their influence on global decision-making and ensure that the interests of emerging economies are adequately represented

China's role for the BRICS Countries

China has a prominent role as an export nation and plays a significant role in the global trade landscape. The country has experienced an impressive rise in recent decades, becoming one of the largest export nations in the world. The export industry has become a major driver of China's economic growth and has a significant impact on the global economy.

China has immense manufacturing capacity, allowing it to produce and export large quantities of goods to the global market. The country has a well-developed industry, particularly in areas such as electronics, clothing, toys, engineering and furniture manufacturing. Chinese companies benefit from efficient production processes, low labor costs and an extensive supply chain, enabling them to offer high-quality products at competitive prices.

China has established extensive trade relations with countries around the world. It is one of the largest exporters of goods to almost all regions of the world. In particular, trade relations between China and developed countries, including the United States and Europe, are of great importance. Chinese products are in demand in the global market due to their competitive prices, but also due to their quality and variety.

China plays an important role in global value chains, particularly in areas such as electronics and automotive. Many international companies have relocated their production to China to benefit from the country's low labor costs and efficient infrastructure. Chinese companies act as suppliers to these global companies and contribute to the final assembly of products that are then exported worldwide.

China's export surplus, that is, the difference between the country's exports and imports, is significant. This has led to China accumulating significant foreign exchange reserves. Foreign exchange reserves enable China to stabilize its currency, make investments abroad, and mitigate financial risks. China's foreign exchange reserves are an important component of global financial stability.

China has also made significant investments in infrastructure projects designed to further promote trade and exports. The most prominent example is the Belt and Road Initiative (BRI), which aims to create trade corridors between China and various regions of the world. By developing ports, roads, railways and other infrastructure, China supports trade with the countries involved and facilitates the exchange of goods.

China has made significant efforts to advance its technological innovation and quality improvement in production. The country has invested in areas such as artificial intelligence, robotics, 5G technology and renewable energy. This has enabled China to move beyond its image as a producer of low-cost, mass-produced goods and focus on developing high-quality, technologically advanced products.

It is important to note that China's role as an export nation also brings with it some challenges. First, China is under pressure to transform its growth model and rely more on domestic consumption in order to make its economy more sustainable. Second, there are concerns about intellectual property, environmental protection and working conditions in some Chinese industries.

Nevertheless, China remains of great importance to the global economy as an export nation. Its ability to produce and deliver large quantities of goods, its extensive trade relations and its ongoing efforts in technological innovation make China a crucial player in the global trading system.

Another phenomenon that stands out in relation to China's influence on the global economy is the global acquisition of technologies and traditional brands by Chinese companies. In recent years, China has increased its investments in foreign technology companies and established brands in order to accelerate its technological progress and strengthen its presence in the global market. This trend has brought both opportunities and challenges.

China has recognized that access to modern technologies and know-how is crucial to increasing its own competetiveness. To achieve this goal, Chinese companies have increased their investments in foreign companies that possess advanced technologies and patents.

Particularly in areas such as semiconductors, artificial intelligence, biotechnology and renewable energy, Chinese companies have entered into strategic partnerships and acquisitions to expand their technological expertise.

Buying heritage brands allows Chinese companies to gain immediate access to established markets and a loyal customer base. This offers the opportunity to leverage existing distribution channels, brand awareness and customer loyalty to distribute their products and services worldwide. Particularly in the consumer goods industry, Chinese companies have acquired heritage brands to strengthen their presence in the global market.

By buying up technologies and heritage brands, Chinese companies can strengthen their competitiveness. They have access to newer technologies and innovative production methods that give them an edge over their competitors. This allows them to produce high-quality products, expand their product lines and adapt their offerings to the needs of the market. By acquiring heritage brands, Chinese companies can also benefit from their established reputation and prestige.

However, the global purchase of technologies and heritage brands by Chinese companies has also raised concerns. Some countries and regions have taken restrictive measures to control the acquisition of sensitive technologies and strategic companies by Chinese investors. Concerns have been raised about the protection of intellecttual property, know-how and national security. It is important that such transactions properly consider the interests of all parties involved.

In addition, the challenge is to find a proper balance between foreign investment and national interests. It is important to ensure that technology transfer is carried out in a fair and transparent manner and that long-term economic stability and sovereignty are maintained.

The global acquisition of technologies and heritage brands by Chinese companies is a remarkable phenomenon that reflects China's pursuit of technological advancement and global presence. By acquiring technologies, Chinese companies can strengthen their competitiveness and develop innovative products and services. The acquisition of heritage brands provides access to established markets and a loyal customer base. Nevertheless, there are also challenges and concerns related to the protection of intellectual property, know-how and national security.

It is important that such transactions are carried out in a fair and transparent manner and that national interests are duly taken into account. The global acquisition of technologies and heritage brands should serve to create a win-win situation in which both Chinese companies and the acquired companies and countries can benefit.

Russia's role for the BRICS Countries

Russia has taken an increasingly assertive role in recent years to act as a counterweight to US dominance in the global arena. This development is the result of a combination of geopolitical and economic factors that have enabled Russia to expand its own power and influence.

Russia sees itself as a counterweight to US dominance in geopolitical affairs. The country has a strong military presence and pursues an active foreign policy to defend its interests and strengthen its position as a global power. Russia has demonstrated its role as a counterweight to the US particularly in international conflicts and crises, such as in Syria, where Russia plays an important role as an ally of the Syrian regime.

Russia is one of the largest producers and exporters of oil and natural gas. This dependence of the global economy on Russian energy exports gives Russia considerable leverage to assert its influence and act as a counterweight to the US. Russia has used its energy policy to establish and maintain economic and political relations with other countries, particularly in Europe. This has allowed Russia to strengthen its position and create alternative trade routes that are not controlled by the US.

Russia has established the Eurasian Economic Union (EAEU) to promote closer economic integration with its neighboring countries. This union, consisting of Russia, Kazakhstan, Belarus, Armenia, and Kyrgyzstan, is intended to serve as a counterweight to other economic blocs such as the European Union. By promoting regional trade and economic cooperation, Russia aims to increase its economic strength and consolidate its position in the global economy.

Russia has increased its participation in multilateral institutions to increase its voice in global affairs and act as a counterweight to US dominance. The country is a member of the UN Security Council and plays an active role in organizations such as the Shanghai Cooperation Organization (SCO) and the BRICS group. Through this participation, Russia aims to strengthen its position and promote a multipolar world order.

Russia has also made efforts to increase its technological independence from the US. The country has invested in areas such as space, defense technology, and information and communications technology to expand its own technological base and reduce its dependence on foreign technology. This allows Russia to ensure its national security and act as a counterweight to U.S. dominance in these areas.

It is important to note that Russia's quest to counterbalance the U.S. has also encountered concerns and tensions in international relations. This has led to conflict and political tensions between Russia and the U.S., particularly in areas such as the Ukraine crisis and foreign election interference. The dynamic between Russia and the U.S. remains an important factor in global geopolitics.

Russia plays a significant role as a supplier of raw materials on the global stage. The country has extensive natural resources and is one of the world's largest producers and exporters of raw materials. This role as a supplier of raw materials has significant influence on the Russian economy and the global economy as a whole.

Russia is one of the largest producers and exporters of oil and natural gas. The country has extensive reserves of conventional and unconventional petroleum and has a well-developed infrastructure for the extraction and transportation of these resources. Russia exports its energy products to various regions of the world, including Europe, Asia and the Middle East. Energy exports contribute significantly to the Russian state budget and are an important factor in global energy security.

Russia has rich deposits of minerals and metals, including iron ore, aluminum, nickel, copper, gold and diamonds. The country is one of the largest producers and exporters of these commodities and plays an important role in global markets. The Russian mining industry has a significant impact on the global availability and prices of these commodities.

Russia is one of the largest producers of uranium, which is used as fuel in the nuclear energy industry. The country exports uranium to various countries that operate nuclear power plants. In addition, Russia has a leading position in nuclear energy technology and is a major supplier of nuclear reactors and services in the global market.

The nuclear energy industry contributes to energy supply and climate protection.

Russia has large forest areas and is one of the largest producers of wood and wood products. The country exports wood, wood pellets and other wood products to various countries. The Russian forestry industry is important not only for the global wood market but also for protecting biodiversity and natural resources in Russian forests.

Russia is also a major producer and exporter of agricultural products such as wheat, barley, sunflower oil, sugar and meat products. The country has significant agricultural potential due to its large arable land and favorable climate. Agricultural exports contribute to food security on a global level.

Russia's role as a raw material supplier has both advantages and challenges. Exports of raw materials bring the country significant revenues and contribute to economic development. At the same time, however, the Russian economy is highly dependent on raw material prices and international market fluctuations, which can lead to economic volatility. In addition, there is the challenge of making raw material exploitation sustainable and minimizing environmental impacts.

Russia's role as a raw materials supplier also has geopolitical implications. The country uses its raw materials resources as a tool for shaping foreign policy and as a lever to exert influence on other countries and regions. Relations between Russia and other countries, especially in terms of energy supply and dependence, are therefore of great importance for geopolitical dynamics.

Russia plays a significant role as a raw materials supplier, especially in the field of energy, minerals, metals and agricultural products. Exports of raw materials contribute significantly to the Russian economy and have an impact on the global economy. At the same time, they pose challenges for Russia in terms of economic volatility and environmental impacts. Russia's role as a raw materials supplier also has geopolitical implications and influences relations with other countries and regions.

But Russia also has a long history as a military counterweight to the United States and plays a significant role in the global security architecture. The country has strong military power and has both conventional and nuclear capabilities, making it a potential adversary of the United States. Russia's military strength has implications for international security and geopolitical relations between the two countries.

Russia is one of the world's two leading nuclear powers, along with the United States. The country has an extensive arsenal of nuclear weapons and pursues a policy of nuclear deterrence. The presence of these nuclear capabilities ensures that Russia is perceived as a potential threat to the United States and plays a role as a military counterweight. The nuclear balance between Russia and the United States has contributed to relative stability in bilateral relations.

Russia has one of the largest and most modern conventional armed forces in the world. The country has a well-equipped army, air force, and navy capable of handling a wide range of missions. Russia has developed its military capabilities through modernization, armament programs, and strategic investments. Russia's conventional forces pose a potential challenge to the United States and can serve as a military counterweight.

Russia has used its military presence to defend its interests in the region and cement its role as a counterweight to the United States. In the former Soviet Union in particular, Russia has conducted military operations, such as in Ukraine and Georgia, to protect its sphere of influence and demonstrate a stronger presence. These regional activities have led to tensions between Russia and the US and influenced geopolitical dynamics.

Russia has also positioned itself as a player in cyber warfare and hybrid threats. The country has reportedly conducted cyber attacks on other countries and attempted to influence political processes in other countries. These activities have led to tensions between Russia and the US and changed the security landscape. Russia's ability to use asymmetric warfare tactics poses a challenge to the US.

Russia has a powerful defense industry that develops and produces modern weapons systems and technologies. The country is a major exporter of defense equipment and supplies various countries around the world. The Russian defense industry has helped increase the country's military strength and cement its position as a counterweight to US dominance in the defense industry.

It is important to note that the military dynamics between Russia and the US are characterized by tensions and complex geopolitical challenges. Both countries have their own national security interests and seek regional and global power projection..

Russia plays a significant role as a military counterweight to the US. The country has nuclear and conventional forces, regional influence, cyber warfare capabilities, and a powerful defense industry. Russia's military strength impacts the geopolitical relations between the two countries and influences the international security architecture. However, the Russia-US relationship remains marked by tensions and conflicts and requires constructive diplomacy and dialogue to ensure security and stability.

Russia has increasingly taken on a role as a counterweight to US dominance on the world stage in recent years. Through geopolitical counterweighting, its role as an energy exporter, the promotion of Eurasian integration, participation in multilateral institutions, and the strengthening of technological independence, Russia has sought to increase its own power and influence. However, the relationship between Russia and the US remains marked by tension and conflict, and the dynamics between the two countries will continue to influence global geopolitics.

Brazil's role for the BRICS Countries

Brazil plays an important role within the BRICS and has a significant influence on the dynamics and objectives of this group. As the largest country in South America and one of the largest economies in the world, Brazil brings a variety of resources and strengths to the BRICS.

Brazil has a diverse and robust economy based on various sectors. The country is a major producer and exporter of commodities such as agricultural products, petroleum, iron and steel. In addition, Brazil has a well-developed industry in areas such as automobile manufacturing, mechanical engineering, chemicals and electronics. The Brazilian economy is a major driver of the growth and stability of the BRICS.

Brazil is one of the largest producers and exporters of agricultural products in the world. The country has a large arable land area and a favorable climate, which leads to high productivity in the agricultural industry. Brazil is a leading producer of soybeans, coffee, sugar cane, oranges, beef and poultry. Brazil's agricultural and food production plays an important role in food security and global trade.

Brazil has also made significant progress in developing renewable energy. The country is one of the largest producers of bioethanol, which is derived from sugar cane. Brazil has reduced its dependence on fossil fuels and is increasingly relying on renewable energy such as hydropower, biomass and solar energy. Brazil has developed innovative technologies and practices in the use of renewable energy and is playing an important role in the global energy transition.

Brazil is home to a large part of the Amazon rainforest, which is considered the "lungs of the world". The country is committed to protecting the environment and biodiversity and is taking measures to curb deforestation, protect indigenous territories and promote sustainable land use. Brazil plays an important role in global environmental initiatives and brings its experience and expertise to the BRICS context.

Brazil has made significant investments in infrastructure projects to promote its economic development and connectivity. The country has invested in the expansion of transport systems, ports, airports and energy infrastructure. These investments create new opportunities for trade and cooperation within the BRICS countries and contribute to regional integration.

Brazil brings its specific strengths and resources to the BRICS and helps strengthen cooperation and exchanges within this group. By promoting trade, investment, technology exchange and cultural dialogue, Brazil contributes to strengthening BRICS initiatives and promotes the growth and development of all member countries.

Brazil plays a crucial role within the BRICS. The country brings a strong economy, significant agricultural and food production, expertise in renewable energy, a commitment to environmental protection and biodiversity, and extensive investments in infrastructure. Brazil contributes to strengthening cooperation within the BRICS and promotes the growth and development of all member countries.

Brazil also has geopolitical importance for the BRICS, resulting from its geographical location, economic strength and political influence. As the largest country in South America and one of the most populous countries in the world, Brazil plays an important ròle in shaping the regional and global dynamics of the BRICS.

Brazil is the only member of the BRICS in South America, making it a major player in the Latin American region. The country has historical and economic ties with other Latin American countries and acts as a bridge between the BRICS and the Latin American community. Brazil can serve as a facilitator and catalyst for cooperation and integration between the BRICS and other Latin American countries.

Brazil is one of the world's largest economies and has considerable economic potential. The country plays an important role in global trade and is a major exporter of raw materials, agricultural products and manufactured goods. Brazil's economic strength has an impact on the entire BRICS group and helps strengthen economic potential and trade relations within the BRICS.

Brazil has considerable political influence due to its size, population and political structure. The country plays an active role in regional and global forums such as the United Nations and the Organization of American States. Brazil's political influence within the BRICS can help strengthen common positions, address political challenges, and influence global governance.

Brazil has a well-equipped army and plays an important role in the regional security architecture. The country has participated in international peacekeeping missions and has been involved in stabilizing conflicts in other countries. Cooperation on security and defense issues within the

BRICS can help address regional security threats and promote common security interests.

Brazil is known for its cultural diversity and diplomatic skills. The country has a rich cultural tradition that allows it to build cultural bridges between the BRICS and other regions. Brazil can act as a mediator in diplomatic disputes and help promote intercultural exchanges within the BRICS.

Brazil's geopolitical importance to the BRICS lies in its ability to act as a mediator, economic driver, and political actor. Through its regional leadership, economic strength, political influence, security cooperation and diplomatic capabilities, Brazil contributes to strengthening BRICS initiatives and promotes cooperation and exchanges within the group.

Brazil has geopolitical importance for the BRICS countries, which derives from its geographical location, economic strength, political influence and diplomatic capacity. The country plays an important role as a bridge between the BRICS countries and the Latin American community and contributes to the regional and global dynamics of the BRICS group. Brazil can act as a mediator, economic engine and political actor, helping to promote the goals and interests of the BRICS countries.

India's role for the BRICS Countries

India plays a significant role within the BRICS and brings various elements to the group that underline its importance. As the most populous country and one of the largest economies in the world, India has a significant impact on the dynamics and objectives of the BRICS.

India has an immense population, which means a large workforce and human capital. This demographic strength offers enormous potential for economic growth and development. India's workforce is a key resource for the BRICS and contributes to their economic dynamism and innovation.

India is an emerging economy and is experiencing stable economic growth. The country has a broad economic base that includes various sectors such as information technology, pharmaceuticals, automotive, services and agriculture. India's economic strength contributes to the development and strengthening of the BRICS and opens up new opportunities for trade, investment and economic cooperation.

India has emerged as a major player in the global technology and IT industry. The country is known for its technology companies, software development and digital innovations. India contributes to the technological development of the BRICS and promotes the exchange of expertise and technological advancement within the group.

India plays a leading role in South Asia and influences the geopolitical dynamics in the region. The country has close political, economic and cultural ties with other countries in South Asia. India can serve as a facilitator and catalyst for cooperation and integration within the BRICS and South Asia.

India is committed to promoting sustainable development and addressing environmental concerns. The country has launched initiatives to promote renewable energy, combat pollution and improve sustainability in various sectors. India's efforts in sustainable development and environmental protection contribute to the common agenda of the BRICS and promote the exchange of best practices.

The importance of India to the BRICS lies in its population strength, economic potency, technological innovation, regional leadership and sustainable development initiateves. India brings a variety of resources and strengths to the group and helps strengthen the BRICS initiatives.

India plays a prominent economic role within the BRICS and is a key contributor to the strengthening and dynamism of this group. As one of the largest economies in the world and an emerging market, India brings a variety of economic resources and strengths to the BRICS.

India has a huge domestic market with a growing middle class and increasing consumption potential. The purchasing power of the Indian population drives domestic economic growth and offers a huge sales opportunity for companies within the BRICS. India's growing consumer sector is attractive for foreign investment and helps strengthen the BRICS economies.

India is known for its thriving services industry, particularly in the area of information technology and IT-enabled services. The country is a global outsourcing hub and offers high-quality services in the areas of software development, IT consulting, business process outsourcing and digital innovations. India's expertise in the services sector helps strengthen the BRICS economies and promotes the exchange of knowledge and skilled workers within the group.

India has a diverse manufacturing industry ranging from automobiles to pharmaceuticals and electronics. The country is one of the largest exporters of pharmaceutical products and textiles. India's manufacturing sector has a strong export orientation and helps increase trade activities within the BRICS countries. India plays an important role as a manufacturer and supplier of products to the BRICS markets and beyond.

India has made extensive investments in infrastructure projects to promote economic development and connectivity at home and abroad. The country is investing in expanding transport networks, energy infrastructure, digital infrastructure and urban development. India's infrastructure initiatives provide opportunities for investment and economic cooperation within the BRICS countries and support regional integration.

India is one of the largest producers of agricultural products and foodstuffs. The country has a wide range of agricultural products including rice, wheat, sugar, dairy products and spices.

India's agricultural sector contributes to food security and promotes agricultural trade within the BRICS.

India's economic role for the BRICS lies in its size, domestic market, services sector, manufacturing industry, investment in infrastructure and agricultural production. India offers opportunities for trade, investment, technological exchange and economic cooperation within the BRICS group.

India plays a prominent economic role within the BRICS. The country brings to the group a large domestic market, a thriving services sector, a diverse manufacturing industry, investment in infrastructure and strong agricultural production. India contributes to strengthening the BRICS economies, promotes trade, investment and technological exchange and offers opportunities for economic cooperation and integration within the group.

India plays a significant role within the BRICS. The country brings to the group a large population, an emerging economy, technological innovations, regional leadership and efforts towards sustainable development. India contributes to the development and strengthening of the BRICS countries and promotes cooperation in the areas of trade, investment, technology and sustainability.

India plays a geopolitical role that is of great importance to the BRICS. India's geopolitical position, size and political objectives influence the dynamics and objectives of the BRICS group in many ways.

India plays a leading role in South Asia and has significant influence on the geopolitical dynamics in the region. The country maintains close political, economic and cultural ties with neighboring countries and plays an active role in regional organizations such as the South Asian Association for Regional Cooperation (SAARC). India's regional leadership in South Asia impacts the BRICS and can serve as a catalyst for regional integration and cooperation.

India has an active foreign policy and is committed to multilateral cooperation. The country is involved in various international forums such as the United Nations, the World Trade Organization and the Paris Climate Agreement. India's diplomatic efforts help represent the interests of the BRICS at the global level and promote cooperation in the areas of trade, climate change, security and development.

India has conflict-ridden situations on various borders, particularly with China and Pakistan. These border disputes have an impact on the geopolitical dynamics of the BRICS group. India is committed to territorial integrity and security and works with the BRICS countries to promote common security interests and resolve disputes peacefully.

India has a strong interest in maritime security and maritime trade as it has a long coastline and strategically important sea routes. The country is committed to protecting its maritime interests and maintaining a stable maritime trade environment. India can work with the BRICS countries to advance maritime security initiatives and help promote maritime trade.

India is one of the largest energy consumers in the world and has a strong interest in energy security and addressing climate change. The country is working to achieve a balanced energy supply by developing renewable energy and access to energy sources. India can work with the BRICS countries to advance initiatives to promote renewable energy, energy efficiency and combat climate change.

India's geopolitical role for the BRICS lies in its regional leadership, active foreign policy, involvement in security issues, maritime interests and commitment to energy security and climate change. India contributes to geopolitical stability and cooperation within the BRICS group and promotes common interests at the regional and global levels.

India plays a geopolitical role of great importance for the BRICS. The country brings regional leadership, active foreign policy, involvement in security issues, maritime interests and a strong commitment to energy security and climate change to the group. India contributes to geopolitical stability and cooperation within the BRICS group and promotes common interests in trade, security, energy and the environment.

South Africa's role within the BRICS Countries

South Africa plays an important role within the BRICS and brings a unique perspective and strengths to the group. As the only African nation in the BRICS group, South Africa has a number of aspects that shape its role for the BRICS.

South Africa takes a leading role in Africa and has worked to promote African integration and cooperation. The country is a member of the African Union and plays an active role in regional organizations such as the Southern African Development Community (SADC). South Africa can act as a facilitator and catalyst for cooperation and integration between the BRICS and other African countries.

South Africa is one of the largest economies in Africa and brings considerable economic potential to the BRICS. The country has a diverse economy based on mining, manufacturing, financial services, tourism and information technology. South Africa has also made investments in infrastructure projects to promote its economic development and improve regional connectivity. South Africa's economic strength helps strengthen the BRICS economies.

South Africa is rich in natural resources, particularly minerals such as gold, platinum, coal and diamonds. The country also has significant deposits of renewable energy resources such as solar and wind. South Africa's resource wealth and commitment to developing renewable energy are important to the BRICS and provide opportunities for trade, investment and technological exchange in the mining and energy sectors.

South Africa is actively involved in development cooperation and provides humanitarian assistance in various African countries. The country promotes the exchange of expertise, education, healthcare and infrastructure projects to support growth and development in the region. South Africa's development cooperation can serve as a model for cooperation between the BRICS and other developing countries.

South Africa is known for its cultural diversity, its history of fighting apartheid and its diplomacy. The country has a long tradition of mediation and dialogue and brings these skills to the BRICS. South Africa can act as a cultural mediator and advocate for peace, justice and inclusion within the BRICS group.

South Africa plays an important role as a bridge between the BRICS and the African continent. Through its regional leadership, economic strength, natural resources, commitment to development cooperation and cultural diversity, South Africa contributes to strengthening BRICS initiatives and promotes cooperation and exchanges within the group.

South Africa plays a significant economic role within the BRICS and contributes to the strengthening and dynamism of the group. The country brings a number of economic resources and strengths to the BRICS that underline its economic importance.

South Africa is rich in natural resources and has a long history of mining. The country is one of the world's largest producers of minerals such as gold, platinum, diamonds, coal and manganese. South Africa's extractive industries are important to the BRICS as they provide raw materials for production and trade. South Africa contributes to securing the supply of raw materials and diversifying the BRICS economies.

South Africa has a developed manufacturing industry, particularly in the automotive sector. The country is home to major automotive manufacturers engaged in the production of vehicles and components. South Africa's automotive sector provides jobs and promotes technological advancement. South Africa's manufacturing industry plays an important role in trade and cooperation within the BRICS.

South Africa has a developed services sector that includes areas such as finance, tourism, telecommunications and information technology. The country has a well-established stock exchange and is a regional financial centre. South Africa's financial services support trade and investment within the BRICS and help strengthen the BRICS economies.

South Africa is a popular tourist destination with rich natural and cultural diversity. The country offers a wide range of tourism attractions, including game reserves, stunning landscapes and cultural sites. The tourism sector in South Africa contributes to economic development and the exchange of people and cultures within the BRICS.

South Africa has made investments in infrastructure projects to support its economic development and improve regional connectivity. The country has a well-developed transport infrastructure, including roads, ports and airports. South Africa has also developed renewable energy resources such as solar and wind power and plays a role in promoting renewable energy within the BRICS.

South Africa's economic role for the BRICS lies in its commodity production, manufacturing industry, services, tourism sector, infrastructure development and participation in renewable energy. South Africa helps strengthen the BRICS economies, promotes trade, investment and technological cooperation within the group.

South Africa plays a significant economic role within the BRICS. The country brings a variety of resources and strengths to the group, including commodities, a developed manufacturing industry, services, tourism sector, infrastructure and renewable energy. South Africa helps strengthen the BRICS economies, promotes trade, investment and technological cooperation and provides opportunities for economic integration and development within the group.

But South Africa also plays an important geopolitical role of great importance to the BRICS and contributes to the strengthening of the group. The country brings a unique perspective and strengths to the BRICS that underline its geopolitical importance.

South Africa plays a leading role in Africa and has a strong voice in regional and international forums. The country is an active member of the African Union (AU) and plays an important role in regional organizations such as the Southern African Development Community (SADC). South Africa can act as a bridge between the BRICS and the African continent and help promote African integration and cooperation.

South Africa pursues an active foreign policy and is engaged at the international level. The country has a long history of diplomatic engagement and is committed to peace, security, human rights and development. South Africa can act as a diplomatic actor within the BRICS and represent common positions on global challenges.

South Africa has a long tradition of peacekeeping and conflict resolution, particularly on the African continent. The country has participated in various United Nations peacekeeping missions and played an important role in mediating and resolving conflicts. South Africa can act as a peacekeeping and conflict resolution actor within the BRICS and contribute to stability in the region.

South Africa has abundant natural resources, particularly minerals and raw materials. The country also has significant deposits of renewable energy resources such as solar and wind. South Africa's resource security and energy cooperation are important to the BRICS and provide opportunities for trade, investment and technological exchange in the mining and energy sectors.

South Africa is actively engaged in development cooperation and promotes cooperation between the BRICS and other developing countries. The country provides technical assistance, expertise and financial assistance to promote growth and development in other African countries. South Africa's development cooperation can serve as a model for cooperation between the BRICS and other developing countries.

South Africa's geopolitical role for the BRICS lies in its African leadership, diplomatic engagement, peacekeeping and conflict resolution, resource security, development cooperation and participation in energy cooperation. South Africa contributes to geopolitical stability and cooperation within the BRICS group and promotes common interests at the regional and global level.

South Africa brings African leadership, diplomatic engagement, peacekeeping, resource security, development cooperation and energy cooperation to the group. South Africa contributes to geopolitical stability and cooperation within the BRICS group and promotes common interests in the areas of peace, security, trade and development.

South Africa plays a significant role within the BRICS countries overall. The country brings regional leadership, a strong economy, natural resources, commitment to development cooperation and cultural diversity to the group. South Africa can serve as a bridge between the BRICS countries and the African continent and contribute to strengthening cooperation, integration and development within the group.

Geostrategically, the BRICS countries are geographically spread across different continents. This has immense political significance spread across the entire world. The geographical distribution of the BRICS countries is reflected in their diversity and their ability to bring different geopolitical perspectives. This leads to a beneficial diversity of perspectives on overall political processes, but also to a strategic distribution of spheres of influence. At the same time, however, this can also have the potential for conflicts of interest within the BRICS community.

Located in South America, Brazil is the largest country in the continent. It borders many other South American countries and has outstanding political importance in the region. Brazil brings its experience as the largest economy in Latin America and as a regional power to the BRICS group. The country also plays a role in promoting integration and cooperation in South America.

Stretching across Europe and Asia, Russia is the world's largest country by area. It holds an important geopolitical position as a bridge between Eastern and Western Europe and a link between Asia and Europe. Russia is a major global power with political and military influence. It brings its extensive resources and geopolitical experience to the BRICS group and plays a role in promoting cooperation between Europe and Asia.

Located in southern Asia, India covers a large area of the Indian subcontinent. It has a strategic location at the crossroads of South Asia, Central Asia and the Middle East. India is an emerging power with one of the world's largest populations and a rapidly growing economy. It brings its demographic strength, regional leadership and cultural diversity to the BRICS group and plays an important role in promoting cooperation in South Asia.

Located in East Asia, China is the world's most populous country and has outstanding geopolitical importance in the region and beyond. China is an emerging superpower with one of the world's largest economies and strong political influence. The country brings its economic strength, technological innovations and political leadership to the BRICS group. China plays a central role in promoting cooperation in East Asia and strengthening the multilateral system.

Located in Southern Africa, South Africa is the only African country in the BRICS group. It has an important geopolitical position on the African continent and helps promote cooperation in Africa. South Africa brings its experience in regional leadership, economic strength, resources and cultural diversity to the BRICS group.

The geographical distribution of the BRICS countries reflects the immense reach of their political importance. As countries with different geographical positions and geopolitical experiences, the BRICS bring diverse perspectives to the group. They play an important role in shaping global governance structures, promoting the multilateral trading system, strengthening South-South cooperation and representing common interests at the regional and international levels.

The geographical distribution of the BRICS countries also has geostrategic significance. Their geographical positioning enables them to pursue common interests worldwide and strengthen their influence at the global level.

The geostrategic significance of the BRICS countries lies in their ability to pursue common interests, promote regional stability, ensure access to key trade routes and serve as intermediaries between different political and economic actors. The BRICS countries can use their geostrategic position to achieve their political goals at the global level and strengthen their voice in international forums.

Their positioning enables them to pursue common interests, promote regional stability and strengthen their influence at the global level. Brazil, Russia, India, China and South Africa use their geostrategic advantages to achieve their political goals and strengthen their role in international affairs.

The geostrategic distribution of the BRICS countries can be seen as a counterweight to the US spheres of influence. Each BRICS country brings a unique geostrategic position that allows the group to achieve a stronger presence and influence on a global level.

The geostrategic distribution of the BRICS countries as a counterweight to the US spheres of influence allows the group to have a stronger voice on a global level and defend common interests. Through their geostrategic positions, the BRICS countries can promote a multipolar world order and advance alternative political and economic models that differ from the US-dominated systems.

The BRICS countries are committed to a multipolar world order. Their geostrategic positioning allows them to have a stronger presence on a global level and to make more independent decisions that differ from the US interests.

The BRICS countries serve as important players in shaping the global political landscape and promoting a more balanced distribution of power and influence in the world.

Overall, the BRICS countries undoubtedly have a significant impact on the global economy. Their impressive economic growth, growing trade relations, technological innovations and efforts towards fairer global governance have helped to change global economic and political dynamics. By continuing to build on their strengths, addressing challenges and promoting cooperation, the BRICS countries can further consolidate their position as important players in the global economy and contribute to sustainable development.

In recent years, several countries have expressed interest in joining the BRICS and some have formally applied or been officially invited. The newest members, set to join on January 1, 2024, include major oil-producing countries such as Egypt, Iran, Saudi Arabia, United Arab Emirates. But other countries such as Argentina and Ethiopia have also applied.

These countries have different motivations for joining BRICS:

Economic diversification and cooperation: The BRICS bloc provides a platform to promote economic cooperation, trade and investment among member countries. Countries like Saudi Arabia and the United Arab Emirates may be interested in diversifying their economies and no longer being solely dependent on oil and gas exports.

Strengthening geopolitical position: By joining an influential international bloc, countries can strengthen their geopolitical position. Iran and Egypt, for example, may seek to increase their influence on a global level and expand their diplomatic networks.

Access to markets and investments: Countries like Argentina and Ethiopia could benefit from increased trade opportunities and foreign direct investment promoted by cooperation with BRICS countries.

Multilateral cooperation: BRICS provides a platform for multilateral cooperation in various fields such as science and technology, education and infrastructure development. This cooperation can support the development and modernization of member countries.

Alternative to Western dominance: Some countries may see BRICS as a counterweight to the economic and political dominance of Western countries and institutions such as the World Bank and the International Monetary Fund (IMF). This is especially true for countries like Iran, which suffer from Western sanctions.

The expansion of BRICS reflects the growing interest of many countries in exploring alternative forms of international cooperation that may better support their own development goals and provide them with greater independence in the global arena.

The geopolitical implications of the BRICS Countries

The BRICS are known for their huge populations, economic potential and strategic importance. Their geographical spread across different continents gives them a unique geopolitical position. Together, the BRICS represent about 40% of the world's population and nearly 30% of the global land mass.

An important aspect of the geopolitical implications of the BRICS is their economic strength. Brazil, Russia, India, China and South Africa have extensive natural resources, a growing middle class and a large domestic market. Their combined economic output has increased significantly in recent years and is expected to continue to grow.

This economic strength has given the BRICS greater bargaining power on the international stage. They can use their economic resources to conclude trade deals, exert political influence and promote their interests. The establishment of the New Development Bank (NDB) by the BRICS, which serves as an alternative to the World Bank and the International Monetary Fund (IMF), gives the BRICS countries more say in the global financial architecture.

Another important issue related to the geopolitical implications of the BRICS is their increasing role as political actors. These emerging powers are striving to create a multipolar world order that challenges the dominance of Western countries. They advocate for a stronger voice for developing countries in global affairs and call for reform of existing international institutions.

The BRICS countries have various political goals that demonstrate their influence at the regional and global levels. For example, Brazil seeks a greater role in Latin America and is committed to promoting democracy and human rights. Russia has increased its military presence in the region and is trying to expand its influence in the Eurasian region. India is seeking a greater leadership role in South Asia and has pursued an active foreign policy to promote its national interests. China has emerged as a global superpower and aspires to play a dominant role in Asia and Africa. South Africa is committed to promoting peace and stability on the African continent and is actively involved in regional organizations such as the African Union.

The BRICS countries also have geopolitical implications in terms of international security issues. Their growing influence impacts global power relations and can lead to tensions and conflicts. In particular, the strategic competition between China and the USA is seen as a potential geopolitical conflict, as both countries compete for influence and dominance in different regions.

In addition, the BRICS countries have taken on an important role in global development issues. They have committed to promoting sustainable development and poverty reduction, for example in Africa. Through their economic cooperation and development aid, the BRICS countries contribute to strengthening developing countries and calling for a fairer world order.

The geopolitical implications of the BRICS countries are diverse and complex. Their growing influence in the global economy and politics impacts existing global power structures. While some see the BRICS countries as a positive force for promoting a multipolar world order, others see them as a challenge to the dominance of Western countries. The future will tell how the geopolitical landscape evolves and how the BRICS will consolidate their position and influence in the world.

The BRICS have assumed an increasingly larger role in the global geopolitical arena in recent years. Their geographical spread across different continents gives them a unique geopolitical position.

An important aspect of the geopolitical implications of the BRICS is their economic strength. Brazil, Russia, India, China and South Africa have extensive natural resources, a growing middle class and a large domestic market. Their combined economic output has increased significantly in recent years and is expected to continue to grow.

They can use their economic resources to enter into trade deals, exert political influence, and promote their interests. Another important issue related to the geopolitical implications of the BRICS is their increasing role as political actors. These emerging powers are striving to create a multipolar world order that challenges the dominance of Western countries. They advocate for a stronger voice for developing countries in global affairs and call for reform of existing international institutions.

The BRICS have various political goals that demonstrate their influence at the regional and global levels. For example, Brazil is seeking a larger role in Latin America and is committed to promoting democracy and human rights. Russia has increased its military presence in the region and is trying to expand its influence in the Eurasian region. India is seeking a greater leadership role in South Asia and has pursued an active foreign policy to promote its national interests. China has emerged as a global superpower and is striving to play a dominant role in Asia and Africa. South Africa is committed to promoting peace and stability on the African continent and is actively involved in regional organizations such as the African Union.

The BRICS countries also have geopolitical implications in terms of international security issues. Their growing influence impacts global power relations and can lead to tensions and conflicts. In particular, the strategic competition between China and the US is seen as a potential geopolitical conflict as both countries compete for influence and dominance in different regions.

The dwindling economic influence of the US in developing countries can be attributed to several negative aspects. The US is known for its protectionism and high trade barriers, especially in areas such as agriculture and textiles. Developing countries have difficulty exporting their products to the US market, while at the same time cheap US goods compete with local markets. This has led to an imbalance in trade and has hampered economic development in developing countries.

In parallel, the US is a major consumer of natural resources. In some developing countries, US companies have a reputation for exploiting natural resources such as oil, gas or minerals, often at low prices and by exploiting local labor. This can lead to environmental damage, social injustice and unfair economic conditions.

One example is the influence of the company Monsanto on African agriculture.

The use of Monsanto seed varieties, especially genetically modified varieties, may have resulted in higher yields in the short term, which helped to increase agricultural productivity. But the ultimate result was that African farmers became dependent on a single company. This led to a lack of seed diversity and a massive increase in the cost of seed. This in turn presented smaller farmers with financial challenges and dependence.

The use of Monsanto seed is often accompanied by a "necessary" use of Monsanto herbicides and pesticides. This increases dependency and has had massive negative effects on the environment and the health of farmers.

Monsanto's influence has led to the displacement of millennia-old and proven agricultural practices and the transition to more capital-intensive farming methods, which in turn led to social inequality and disadvantaged smaller farmers.

There have been cases where Monsanto has taken legal action against farmers in Africa when genetically modified seeds were inadvertently found in their fields. These legal disputes have placed financial strains on farmers and caused tensions between Monsanto and the local farming community.

China has been one of the largest donors of development aid in Africa for many years. For example, China has funded a variety of infrastructure projects in Africa, including roads, bridges, ports, railways and airports. A well-known example is the TAZARA railway, which connects Tanzania with Zambia and was funded and built by China.

In addition, China has also helped develop energy infrastructure in Africa. This includes the construction of hydroelectric power plants, solar power plants and wind farms. For example, Africa's largest hydroelectric power plant, which Ethiopia is financially supporting, was built by China.

But China also supports African countries in agriculture to increase agricultural production and improve food security. This includes building irrigation systems, providing agricultural machinery and training for African farmers.

China offers scholarships for African students to study in China. In addition, China has sent medical professionals to Africa to help fight diseases such as Ebola.

Overall, China has taken various measures to promote trade with African countries. These include trade agreements, investment facilitation and the promotion of African exports to China.

It is important to note that there are also controversial aspects to Chinese development aid in Africa, such as concerns about the high level of indebtedness of African countries and the conditions attached to Chinese loans. In addition, China's state capitalism always represents its own goals and interests.

For example, by developing African infrastructure, China gains better access to natural resources in Africa. The continent is rich in raw materials such as oil, gas, minerals and agricultural products. By supporting infrastructure projects in Africa, China gains access to these resources, which are important for its own economic development.

It also opens the African market to Chinese products. By building infrastructure projects such as roads, bridges, ports and telecommunications networks in Africa, China creates a market for its products and increases its export opportunities.

China also uses its development aid in Africa to gain political support from African countries at the international level. Through generous aid programs, China strengthens its relations with African governments and increases its political influence in international organizations.

China invests in strategically important areas of Africa to expand its influence in the region. These include, for example, ports, railway lines and other infrastructure projects that allow China to have a stronger presence in Africa and serve as a basis for future economic and political cooperation.

It is therefore important to note that these benefits are not without controversy. There is criticism of Chinese development aid because it is sometimes tied to conditions that do not always benefit African countries and can lead to indebtedness. In addition, the environmental sustainability of many Chinese projects is also questioned.

So we see that the geopolitical implications of the BRICS countries are diverse and complex. Their growing influence in the world economy and politics has an impact on existing global power structures. While some see the BRICS as a positive force for promoting a multipolar world order, others see them as a challenge to the dominance of Western countries. Time will tell how the geopolitical landscape evolves and how the BRICS will consolidate their position and influence in the world.

The differences in the influence of the US and the BRICS on third countries are significant, as mentioned above, and reflect different geopolitical approaches and interests.

The United States of America has played a dominant role in international politics and economics since the end of World War II. Its influence is based on several factors, including its military strength, economic power, cultural dominance, and diplomatic relations.

The US uses its military strength to secure and promote its interests and values worldwide. It has an extensive network of military bases around the world and is involved in numerous conflicts and military missions. Through its military presence and ability to take rapid military action, the US can exert considerable pressure on third countries and force them to comply with its policies.

In addition, the US uses its economic power to exert influence on third countries. It is the largest economy in the world and has a strong position in global financial institutions such as the International Monetary Fund (IMF) and the World Bank. The US can impose economic sanctions, conclude trade agreements and provide development aid to advance its interests and influence third countries.

Another aspect of US influence lies in its cultural dominance. Through its film industry, music, fashion and other cultural exports, the US has broad global appeal and can carry its values and norms to other countries. This can lead to the assimilation of other cultures and increase US influence on third countries.

The US is also heavily involved diplomatically. It is a founding member of the United Nations and plays a leading role in many international organizations.

Through its diplomatic channels, the US can build alliances, negotiate international agreements, and exert political pressure on third countries.

On the other hand, the BRICS countries have a different approach to influencing third countries. Although they do not have the same long history and global dominance as the US, the BRICS countries have nevertheless gained considerable weight in the international arena.

The BRICS countries rely on economic cooperation and development aid as instruments of influence. China, for example, has become the largest trading partner of many developing countries and has made massive investments in infrastructure projects. Through this economic cooperation, the BRICS countries can gain political influence and promote their interests in the countries concerned.

Another aspect is the promotion of South-South cooperation. The BRICS countries have launched initiatives such as the BRICS Development Bank and the BRICS Sovereign Wealth Fund to strengthen economic cooperation among themselves and with other developing countries. By sharing know-how, technology and resources, the BRICS countries can increase their political weight and act as an alternative to Western institutions.

Politically, the BRICS countries are looking for a multipolar world order in which the voices of developing countries are more heard. They are committed to reforming existing international institutions to achieve fairer representation and decision-making. Through their joint statements and votes in international forums such as the United Nations, the BRICS countries try to represent a coherent political position and promote their interests.

It is important to note that the influence of the BRICS countries differs in some regions and countries. For example, China is particularly active in Africa, while Brazil has close relations with Latin America. Each BRICS country has its own specific interests and priorities, but overall they work together to strengthen their political and economic position in the global arena.

To sum up, the US and the BRICS countries have different approaches and tools to influence third countries. The US relies on military strength, economic pressure, cultural dominance and diplomatic relations, while the BRICS countries rely on economic cooperation, development assistance and political coordination. Both actors have significant influence, but their strategies and priorities differ depending on their geopolitical context and global ambitions. Nevertheless, it is important to remember that on both sides this is a struggle for resources, fought on financial, economic and political grounds.

Security and independence of the BRICS Countries

The BRICS countries are a group of emerging economies that have gained considerable influence on the world stage in recent decades. In addition to their economic potential, their political security and independence are also increasingly becoming the subject of discussion and analysis. In this comprehensive text, we will examine the various aspects of the security and independence of the BRICS countries. From geopolitical factors to economic dependencies and internal challenges, we will provide a detailed insight into the situation of the BRICS countries.

The great importance of these security issues is exemplified by the example of Muammar al-Gaddafi, the former head of government of Libya. He was known for his efforts to introduce an independent gold dinar. This idea was part of his vision to free African countries from Western influence on the economy and to regain control over their own resources.

Gaddafi believed that the international financial market was dominated by Western countries - especially the USA - and that this led to injustice and dependence. He believed that an independent currency based on gold could protect African countries from the effects of the global financial crisis.

In 2009, at an African Union summit, Gaddafi proposed the introduction of a common African currency based on gold. He advocated using the Gold Dinar as a medium of exchange to reduce dependence on the US dollar and other

Western currencies. This proposal was met with divided opinions among African leaders.

Despite his efforts, Gaddafi could not fully achieve his goal. There were several obstacles, including political and economic opposition from other countries and international sanctions, especially from the US. In addition, the unstable political situation in Libya during the Arab Spring in 2011 led to Gaddafi losing his power and eventually being killed.

But back to the BRICS countries, the geopolitical factors play a crucial role in the security and independence of the BRICS countries. Each country has its own geopolitical challenges and interests that affect their decisions and actions. Brazil, for example, is located in South America and has a long coastline that needs to be protected. Russia, on the other hand, stretches across Eurasia and has numerous borders with other countries, making it vulnerable to geopolitical tensions. In addition, NATO's eastern border is increasingly moving closer to Russia due to the inclusion of former Warsaw Pact countries, and could therefore pose a potential threat to Russia. India and China share a disputed border and have a long history of geopolitical rivalry. South Africa, in turn, has its own challenges on the African continent.

The security and independence of the BRICS countries are also influenced by their geopolitical relations with other countries and regions. The close cooperation of the BRICS countries at the international level, such as their common positions in the United Nations, helps to strengthen their security and independence. At the same time, however, they are also dependent on the decisions and actions of other major powers. The geopolitical dynamics between the BRICS countries and the established global players, especially the US and the European Union, play an important role in their security and independence.

In addition to geopolitical factors, economic dependencies are also of great importance for the BRICS countries. Each country has its own strengths and weaknesses in terms of economy and trade. For example, Brazil is a major exporter of commodities such as soy and coffee, while Russia is known for its energy resources, especially oil and gas. India is an emerging market with a strong service industry, while China is considered the "workshop of the world" and plays a leading role in global manufacturing. South Africa, on the other hand, has a rich minerals and mining industry.

These economic strengths and weaknesses create interdependence between the BRICS countries and other countries. The demand for the BRICS countries' commodities and products in the international market affects their economies and, in turn, their security and independence. Price volatility, trade barriers and geopolitical tensions can affect the economies of the BRICS countries and thus threaten their security.

To reduce these dependencies and strengthen their security, the BRICS countries have taken various measures such as promoting regional trade and diversifying their economies.

In addition to external factors, the BRICS countries also face internal challenges that can affect their security and independence. Each country has its own specific political, economic and social challenges to overcome. For example, Brazil struggles with high crime and social inequality.

Russia faces the challenge of diversifying its economy and reducing dependence on oil and gas. India faces the problem of poverty and social injustice. China has to deal with environmental problems and social tensions. South Africa struggles with unemployment, inequality and the legacy of apartheid.

These internal challenges can affect the stability and security of the BRICS countries. A lack of internal stability can lead to political instability, social unrest and economic weakness, which can threaten the independence of the BRICS countries. To address these challenges, the BRICS countries have taken various measures, such as promoting education, developing infrastructure and creating jobs.

The BRICS countries recognize the importance of regional cooperation for their security and independence. They have created various mechanisms and institutions to promote dialogue and cooperation. One example is the BRICS organization itself, which holds regular summits, ministerial conferences and working groups to achieve common goals and strengthen the security of member countries. These regional cooperation mechanisms also enable the BRICS countries to better represent their interests at the international level and raise their voice in global affairs.

In addition, the BRICS countries have expanded their cooperation in various fields such as trade, investment, science and technology, education, culture and tourism. They have signed agreements and arrangements to facilitate exchanges and cooperation in these areas. By expanding economic and cultural ties, the BRICS countries strive for greater independence from established global players and strengthen their position in the world economy.

The BRICS countries also have their future prospects in mind and are working together to further strengthen their security and independence. They have recognized that sustainable development and balanced growth are crucial to ensure long-term stability and security. Therefore, they are increasing their focus on innovative technologies, green energy and environmental protection to make their economies sustainable and reduce dependence on non-renewable resources.

The BRICS countries have also taken initiatives to promote education, human capital and social development. They recognize that a well-educated population and a strong social fabric are crucial to ensuring security and independence. By investing in educational institutions, research centers and social programs, the BRICS countries aim to make their societies more resilient and future-proof.

Another important aspect of the security and independence of the BRICS countries is the promotion of multilateral cooperation. They strive to play a more active role in international organizations such as the United Nations, the World Trade Organization and other global forums. By raising their voices and representing their interests, the BRICS countries aim to ensure that their concerns and needs are adequately addressed.

The security and independence of the BRICS countries are ultimately influenced by a variety of factors. Geopolitical factors such as territorial boundaries, geopolitical relationships and role in global politics play an important role. Economic dependencies on other countries and regions are also significant. In addition, the BRICS countries face internal challenges that can affect their security and independence. By strengthening regional cooperation, diversifying the economy, promoting education and social development, the BRICS countries can strengthen their security and independence in the long term. It remains to be seen how these factors will evolve in the future and what impact they will have on the BRICS countries.

In summary, the security and independence of the BRICS countries is a complex and multifaceted matter. It is influenced by a combination of geopolitical factors, economic dependencies and internal challenges. However, the BRICS countries recognize the importance of regional cooperation, sustainable development, promoting education and multilateral cooperation for their security and independence. Through their joint efforts and strengthening their ties, the BRICS countries can take a strong and independent position in the changing global order. It will be exciting to see how the BRICS countries develop in the coming years and what role they will play in the world.

The challenges to US-Dollar dominance by the BRICS Countries

The BRICS countries have experienced a remarkable economic rise in recent years. They have strengthened their position in the global economy and raised their voice in international affairs. One of the biggest challenges they currently face is the question of dollar dominance and how they can challenge and overcome it.

Dollar dominance is closely linked to the position of the US dollar as the world's reserve currency. Since the end of World War II, the dollar has played a dominant role in international trade and global financial markets. The benefits of dollar dominance are numerous, but it also poses immense risks and challenges not only for the BRICS countries.

Major US banks such as BlackRock, Vanguard and Goldman Sachs play a significant role in the dominance of the US dollar for various reasons. These banks manage enormous assets and are active worldwide. They invest in various markets and countries, often favoring the US dollar as the preferred currency for transactions. This increases the demand for the US dollar and strengthens its role as a reserve currency.

BlackRock and Vanguard in particular are two of the largest asset managers worldwide. Their mutual funds and ETFs are popular among institutional and retail investors. Since many of these funds are quoted in or invest in US dollars, they also support the dominance of the US dollar.

Goldman Sachs is one of the most well-known investment banks and offers a wide range of financial services. They have a strong presence in the international business world and support transactions in US dollars. Their role as intermediaries and advisors also promotes the use of the US dollar in global financial transactions.

These banks have a strong presence worldwide and play a crucial role in the stability and liquidity of the dollar. They are able to facilitate the trading of US dollar assets and thus have a great influence on the international foreign exchange market. This makes the US dollar attractive and remains the preferred currency for many international transactions.

Although the dominance of the US dollar is not limited to these banks. There are also other players such as central banks, multinational companies and governments that play a role. Nevertheless, due to their size, financial reach and activities, the above-mentioned banks have a significant influence on the use of the US dollar in global finance.

As the dollar is currently the main currency for international trade, many BRICS countries are forced to settle large shares of their goods and services in dollars. This can lead to exchange rate fluctuations and affect the competitiveness of the BRICS economies. In addition, they are also vulnerable to the monetary policy of the United States, as changes in US interest rates and money supply can still have an impact on the BRICS countries.

To overcome dollar dominance, the BRICS countries have taken various measures. One way is to strengthen cooperation in trade and investment and to conclude more bilateral currency agreements. By concluding trade agreements in their own currencies, the BRICS countries can increasingly reduce dependence on the dollar and promote the stability of their currencies.

Another step to challenge dollar dominance is to strengthen regional currency agreements. The BRICS countries have already taken steps to promote trade in their own currencies and reduce the use of the dollar as an intermediate currency. For example, China and Russia have entered into bilateral currency agreements to facilitate trade in their respective currencies. This trend may continue and further weaken the role of the dollar in international trade.

In addition, the BRICS countries have also taken initiatives to develop alternative payment systems. One example is the "Digital Silk Road" project initiated by China. This is a digital payment infrastructure designed to facilitate cross-border trade and promote the use of the renminbi as an international reserve currency. Such initiatives can help challenge the dominance of the dollar and create alternative payment routes.

The Digital Silk Road, also known as the "Digital Silk Road Initiative", is a strategy pushed by the Chinese government to promote digital cooperation and technology exchange between China and other countries.

It is an extension of the historical concept of the Silk Road, which was a network of trade routes between Asia, Europe and Africa.

The Digital Silk Road aims to promote the development of digital infrastructure, the exchange of information and innovation, and cooperation in the field of the digital economy. This includes various initiatives such as the construction of fiber optic cable networks, the promotion of 5G technology, the development of e-commerce platforms and the exchange of digital payment systems.

The project aims to strengthen economic integration between China and other countries and facilitate digital trade and communication. It is also seen as a tool to promote Chinese soft power and serves to strengthen China's economic and political ties.

The Digital Silk Road is not without controversy, however. Critics fear that China could exploit its technological dominance and establish a form of digital hegemony. There are also concerns about security and privacy related to Chinese technology firms involved in the project.

However, it is important to note that the challenges to dollar dominance by the BRICS are not without obstacles. The dollar still enjoys a strong reputation as a stable currency and international reserve currency. In addition, the BRICS themselves have different economic and political interests that could limit their cooperation.

Despite these challenges, it is clear that the BRICS are eager to strengthen their position in the global economy and challenge dollar dominance. By deepening their cooperation, concluding bilateral trade agreements and developing alternative payment systems, they can reduce dependence on the dollar and strengthen their own currencies.

The future of dollar dominance therefore depends on many factors, including developments in the BRICS, international acceptance of alternative currencies and the willingness of other countries to challenge dollar dominance. It remains to be seen how this dynamic will unfold in the coming years and whether the BRICS will be successful in meeting the challenges to dollar dominance.

The BRICS countries have increased their efforts in recent years to continue to weaken dollar dominance, but they have encountered various internal challenges that need to be addressed.

One of the challenges is to develop a common strategy and reconcile the different interests of the BRICS countries. Although they are jointly challenging dollar dominance, they still have different economic and political goals. Brazil and Russia, for example, are heavily dependent on their commodity exports, while China and India, as emerging industrial powers, have a greater interest in a stronger role for their own currencies. These different interests can lead to tensions and difficulties in implementing a common strategy.

Another obstacle lies in the stability of the BRICS countries' own currencies. To challenge dollar dominance, their currencies must be trustworthy and stable. Some of the BRICS countries have struggled with currency crises and volatility in the past, which has affected confidence in their currencies. To meet this challenge, they must take measures to strengthen their currencies, improve monetary policy and promote macroeconomic stability.

Furthermore, the BRICS countries must enhance their financial infrastructure capacity. To overcome dollar dominance, they must develop alternative payment and settlement systems that are efficient, secure and reliable.

This requires investing in infrastructure, building clearing houses and developing new technologies. In addition, they must also facilitate access to their financial markets and offer attractive investment opportunities to attract foreign investors.

Another challenge for the BRICS countries is to promote the acceptance of their own currencies in other countries. Although they have already concluded bilateral trade agreements to facilitate trade in their own currencies, they must make further efforts to promote the international use of their currencies. This requires increased cooperation with other countries and the creation of a framework of trust and acceptance for their currencies.

Despite these challenges, the BRICS countries have already made progress in challenging dollar dominance. For example, China has taken steps to establish the renminbi as an international reserve currency. It has entered into bilateral currency agreements with various countries and promoted the use of the renminbi in international trade. In addition, China has also pushed for the establishment of the Asian Infrastructure Investment Bank (AIIB) to create an alternative to the World Bank and the International Monetary Fund.

Russia has also taken steps to reduce dollar dominance. It has increased its gold reserves and promoted trade with other countries in national currencies. Russia has also developed its own international payment system alternative to Visa and Mastercard to be more independent from Western payment systems.

The other BRICS countries have also taken steps to challenge dollar dominance. Brazil has expanded trade with China in national currencies and India has signed bilateral currency agreements with various countries.

Overall, the BRICS countries face major challenges to overcome dollar dominance.

It requires close cooperation, strengthening their currencies, developing financial infrastructure and promoting international acceptance. Nevertheless, the BRICS countries are determined to continue to build their economic strength and create a multipolar world order in which dollar dominance no longer prevails.

The United States has used various methods to address the challenges to dollar dominance posed by the BRICS countries. These measures are designed to preserve the status of the US dollar as the world's reserve currency and maintain its dominance in international trade.

One of the main methods the US uses is to strengthen its own economy and financial system. By having a robust and stable economy, the US can maintain confidence in the dollar and encourage investors to invest in US dollars and buy US securities. The US pursues an expansionary monetary policy to stimulate economic growth and keep inflation under control. This helps to keep the dollar attractive and seen as a safe haven for investment.

In addition, the US also relies on diplomatic and political measures to secure and strengthen its position. It maintains close relations with its allies and partners in the world and promotes the use of the dollar in international trade and financial transactions. The US uses its political and economic power to convince other countries to keep the dollar as a reserve currency and to invest their foreign exchange reserves in dollars. It also strives to maintain and expand its influence in international financial institutions such as the International Monetary Fund (IMF) and the World Bank.

Another tool the US is increasingly using is sanctions. The US uses its position as a global superpower to impose sanctions on countries that threaten its interests or do not support its political agenda. By excluding such countries from international financial systems and prohibiting them from trading in US dollars, the US seeks to demonstrate its power and control over the global financial market and contain potential challenges to dollar dominance.

Furthermore, the US has also taken advantage of its own financial system to maintain dollar dominance. The US is home to the world's largest financial markets, particularly the New York Stock Exchange and Wall Street. It offers a wide range of financial instruments and services that facilitate trading in US dollars. In addition, the US is banking on the use of new technologies such as blockchain and digital payment systems to make international payments more efficient and faster. By doing so, it hopes to cement its leading role in the global financial system.

Another factor contributing to maintaining dollar dominance is the international acceptance of the US dollar as the standard currency for commodity trading, particularly oil. The US has ensured that major oil exporters such as Saudi Arabia and other Gulf countries conduct oil trade in US dollars. This has resulted in a large amount of US dollars flowing into international oil trade and supporting the dollar's status as the main reserve currency.

Overall, the US is using various methods to counter the challenges to dollar dominance posed by the BRICS countries. It is strengthening its own economy, using diplomatic relations and political influence, imposing sanctions, taking advantage of its financial system, and promoting international acceptance of the US dollar. Through these measures, the US is trying to maintain its dominant position in the global economy and overcome the challenges posed by the BRICS countries.

The BRICS countries have realized that in challenging dollar dominance, they may also face obstacles and countermeasures from the US. The US will likely try to defend its dominance and supremacy in the international financial system and curb the influence of the BRICS countries.

One of the possible countermeasures taken by the US is to restrict access to the US financial system. Since the US dollar is the dominant means of payment and many international transactions are processed through the US financial system, the US could try to make it more difficult for the BRICS countries to access this system. This could be done, for example, through restrictive regulations, stricter verification of transactions or the exclusion of certain institutions or countries. Through these measures, the US would try to control trade and financial flows in US dollars and limit the influence of the BRICS countries.

Furthermore, the US can also increasingly resort to political and economic pressure to intimidate the BRICS countries or to deter other countries from cooperating with the BRIS countries. This can be done, for example, by threatening or imposing sanctions against individual

BRICS countries or by using political leverage. The US can try to persuade its allies and partners not to conclude bilateral trade agreements with the BRICS countries or to restrict the use of their own currencies.

Through these measures, the US would seek to isolate the BRICS and complicate their efforts to challenge dollar dominance.

It is important to note that the BRICS are aware of possible countermeasures from the US and are trying to counteract them. They are relying on greater economic cooperation among themselves to reduce their vulnerability to external influences. By expanding trade and investment within the BRICS, they can reduce their dependence on the US financial system and strengthen their own financial infrastructures.

In addition, the BRICS countries are increasingly looking for ways to deepen their cooperation with other countries and regions in order to strengthen their voice and influence in the global financial system.

Despite potential US countermeasures, the BRICS countries are committed to challenging dollar dominance and creating a multipolar world order. They are committed to greater cooperation, developing their own financial infrastructures and promoting international acceptance of their currencies. Although the US will likely try to defend its dominance, the future of dollar dominance is uncertain and depends on developments in the BRICS countries and the global acceptance of alternative currencies.

The role of US big business

The relationship between the United States of America and the BRICS countries has changed significantly over time. US big business in particular plays a significant role in this development. In this chapter, we will look in detail at the role of US big business in dealings with the BRICS countries. We will look at both economic and political aspects and analyze the effects of these relationships.

US big business recognized early on the enormous potential of the BRICS countries and their growing markets. China and India in particular proved to be lucrative targets for investment. The emerging middle classes in these countries offered a high demand for consumer goods and services, which provided US companies with attractive sales markets.

US multinational corporations from various industries, such as technology, financial services, the automotive industry and consumer goods manufacturing, invested heavily in the BRICS markets. They set up subsidiaries, joint ventures and production facilities to benefit from the lower labor costs and strong economic growth in these countries.

In addition, the BRICS countries were also important suppliers of raw materials for US industry. For example, Brazil was a major supplier of agricultural products and raw materials such as soy, coffee and iron ore. Russia had extensive oil and gas reserves, which were of great importance for US energy security.

In addition to economic interests, US big capital also played an important role in exerting political influence in the BRICS countries. Through its financial power, it was able to influence political decision-making processes and create favorable business conditions for US companies.

In some cases, US big capital supported political forces in the BRICS countries that were advantageous to its own interests. It invested in political campaigns and lobbying to promote business-friendly policies that facilitated access to BRICS markets and reduced protectionist measures.

At the same time, US big capital also relied on bilateral and multilateral trade agreements to improve market access and investment protection in the BRICS countries. These agreements often included provisions on intellectual property, market access facilitation, and dispute settlement that benefited U.S. companies.

Despite the economic and political interests of U.S. big business, there were also challenges and tensions in relations with the BRICS countries. One of these was competition with Chinese companies, which also invested heavily in the BRICS markets and represented strong competition for U.S. firms.

In addition, political differences and differing interests led to tensions between the U.S. and some BRICS countries. There were disagreements and conflicts, particularly in the areas of trade, monetary policy, and human rights. These tensions affected business relations and led to uncertainty and risks for U.S. big business.

In recent years, new developments and trends have emerged that have further influenced the role of U.S. big business in its dealings with the BRICS countries. An important aspect is the shift in economic dynamics within the BRICS group. China has established itself as a leading economic power and plays a dominant role in trade relations with the US and other BRICS countries. This has implications for the strategies of US big business, as it needs to focus more on the Chinese market to remain competitive.

Another trend is the increasing importance of technology and innovation. India in particular has become a global hub for technology and IT services. US tech giants such as Google, Apple and Amazon have invested in the Indian market to benefit from the talented workforce and favorable cost structures. These investments have not only brought economic benefits but have also led to closer cooperation between the US and India in the field of technology.

Another important aspect is the geopolitical dynamics between the US and the BRICS countries. In recent years, political relations between the US and Russia have deteriorated, leading to tensions and sanctions. These developments have made the business environment for US companies in Russia more difficult.

At the same time, there have also been political differences between the US and China, particularly in terms of trade and technology. These geopolitical tensions have affected the business environment and created new challenges for US big capital.

The role of US big capital has also had a significant impact on the BRICS countries themselves. On the one hand, the investments and market access by US companies have contributed to economic development and created jobs. The infrastructure projects financed and implemented by

US companies have contributed to modernization and growth.

On the other hand, some BRICS countries have also faced challenges associated with the presence of US big capital. The dependence on foreign investment and technology transfers can make the BRICS countries vulnerable to external economic shocks and political pressures. In addition, the market power of some US companies in some industries has raised concerns about competition and monopoly formation.

In summary, US big capital plays a crucial role in its dealings with the BRICS countries. It has contributed significantly to economic development, exerted political influence and benefited from the opportunities in the BRICS markets. However, the relationship between US big capital and the BRICS countries is also characterized by challenges and tensions arising from geopolitical and economic developments.

The role of US big capital in its dealings with the BRICS countries will continue to be of great importance in the future. Despite current challenges and tensions, interest in the BRICS markets will continue due to their economic potential and increasing importance in the global arena.

US big capital is expected to continue to look for opportunities to expand its presence. At the same time, political and economic developments will impact and bring about changes in US-BRICS relations.

Military and political influence

The dominance of the US dollar as the world's reserve currency is closely linked to the US's military and political influence. Since the end of World War II, the United States has taken a number of measures to establish and maintain the dollar as the preferred currency for international trade and as a reserve of value. These efforts have ranged from diplomatic negotiations to military interventions to protect its interests and consolidate the dollar's influence.

One of the most important initiatives was the creation of the Bretton Woods system in 1944. At the Bretton Woods Conference in New Hampshire, representatives from 44 countries met to lay the foundations for the international monetary system after World War II. The US played a leading role in this and achieved that the US dollar acted as an anchor currency. This meant that the dollar was pegged to gold and other currencies fixed their exchange rate against the dollar. This system gave the dollar a strong position and enabled the US to expand its economic and political power.

The US military presence around the world also played a crucial role in maintaining the dollar's dominance. The United States maintains numerous military bases in strategically important regions and deploys its armed forces to protect its interests. This military influence enabled the US to enforce its political and economic goals and to persuade countries to accept and trade in the dollar.

An example of the link between military and dollar dominance was the Iraq War in 2003. The then Iraqi President Saddam Hussein threatened to settle the sale of oil in euros instead of dollars. This was viewed by the US as a direct threat to the dollar's dominance, as trade in oil is one of the main sources of demand for dollars. The US intervened militarily, overthrowing Saddam Hussein and thus securing its economic interests.

A similar fate befell Muammar al-Gaddafi and the gold dinar. This is another example of a country's efforts to challenge the dollar's dominance. Gaddafi, the former head of government of Libya, played a crucial role in introducing the Gold Dinar as an alternative currency to the dollar. Gaddafi had a long history of opposing the influence of the West, and particularly the United States, in the region. In 2009, he announced his plans to introduce the Gold Dinar, a currency that would be backed by gold and used by African countries. The Gold Dinar was intended to serve as an alternative to the dollar and promote trade among African countries.

The idea behind the Gold Dinar was to free African countries from dependence on the dollar and create an independent currency detached from Western financial markets. Gaddafi argued that the dollar and other reserve currencies weakened African economies and represented a form of economic exploitation. However, the introducetion of the Gold Dinar posed a direct challenge to the dollar, as it had the potential to affect the dollar's value and acceptance as a global reserve currency. Gaddafi hoped that other African countries would follow his example and adopt the Gold Dinar as an alternative to the dollar and other Western currencies.

However, these plans worried the US and other Western countries. The idea that the dollar could be replaced by an alternative currency in any part of the world threatened US supremacy and economic interests. This led to tensions between Gaddafi and the West, which ultimately culminated in military interventions and the overthrow of the Libyan regime in 2011.

There is controversy and various theories as to whether the introduction of the Gold Dinar and Gaddafi's efforts to break free from dollar rule played a direct role in the West's intervention in Libya. Some argue that the West's interests in Libyan oil and geopolitical stability were the main reasons for the intervention. However, others see a direct connection between the threat to the dollar and the military actions against Gaddafi.

Whatever the exact reasons and causes for the intervention in Libya, it is clear that Gaddafi's plans to introduce the gold dinar were suppressed. The dollar remained the dominant reserve currency, and the US supremacy in the global monetary order remained untouched for the time being.

However, the story of Gaddafi and the Gold Dinar illustrates the challenges and risks associated with attempts to undermine the dollar's supremacy. The US has a strong interest in maintaining its position as a leading economic power and issuer of the world's main reserve currency. It is likely to take any action necessary to combat potential threats to the dollar.

It remains to be seen how the global financial landscape will evolve in the coming years. New initiatives and developments could challenge the status quo and promote alternative currencies or systems. The role of Gaddafi and the Gold Dinar in Libya may be a closed chapter, but the question of the dollar's supremacy and the possibilities for alternative currencies remains a relevant topic in today's geopolitical and economic debate.

However, the global financial crisis of 2008 also highlighted the vulnerability of the dollar-based system. The crisis was triggered by a bubble in the US housing market and had severe repercussions for the global economy. This raised doubts about the stability of the dollar and increased the search for alternative currencies and financial systems.

In recent years, various countries, including China and Russia, have made efforts to reduce dependence on the dollar and develop alternative trading mechanisms. China in particular has sought to establish the Chinese yuan as an international reserve currency and to enter into trade agreements that encourage the use of the yuan. These developments could reduce the dollar's influence in the long term.

However, despite these challenges, the dollar remains the dominant reserve currency for now and continues to be viewed by many countries as a safe haven. The U.S. government and the Federal Reserve have taken various measures to maintain confidence in the dollar and ensure the stability of the financial system.

Overall, the U.S. dollar's supremacy is closely linked to U.S. military and political influence. The creation of the Bretton Woods system, promotion of free trade, military presence and political initiatives have enabled the U.S. to establish the dollar as the world's reserve currency in the first place. Although there are challenges and efforts by other countries to undermine the dollar, its supremacy remains for now. The future will show how the global monetary system develops and whether the dollar can maintain its outstanding position.

For their part, the BRICS countries have realized that a dependence on the US dollar limits their economic sovereignty and allows the US to exert pressure to impose its own interests. For this reason, they have started to take measures to reduce the influence of the dollar and develop alternative mechanisms for trade and financing.

Therefore, the BRICS countries have entered into various bilateral agreements to promote trade in their national currencies and reduce the use of the US dollar. A notable example is the agreement between China and Russia in 2014, which allowed direct trade between the Chinese yuan and the Russian ruble. This move was interpreted as an attempt to bypass the US dollar as an intermediary currency in trade relations between the two countries and to strengthen their economic cooperation.

In addition to these economic measures, the BRICS countries have also taken political steps to strengthen their position in global governance and reduce the influence of the US dollar. They have increased their voice in international organizations such as the United Nations and the International Monetary Fund and have sought to promote a multipolar world order in which the BRICS play a larger role.

Another aspect of the BRICS is their growing military influence. China and Russia are the two largest military powers among the BRICS and have made considerable advances in their military capabilities. This has implications for geopolitical dynamics and poses a challenge to US military dominance as well.

China has significantly increased its military spending in recent years and is modernizing its armed forces. The country has built the world's second largest navy and has also made considerable advances in space, cyber warfare and ballistic missiles. This military strength enables China to assert its interests in the region and support its claims in the South China Sea.

Russia has also made significant progress in its military modernization. The country has restructured its armed forces and increased its military presence in the Arctic as well. Russia has also developed its cyber warfare capabilities and has been accused of interfering in other countries' internal affairs. This military strength allows Russia to pursue its geopolitical goals and increase its influence in the world.

The growing military and political strength of the BRICS has led to them being increasingly perceived as a military counterweight to the US. This in turn leads to tensions and conflicts, especially between the US and China. The US views the rise of China as a strategic threat and has increased its military presence in the region. At the same time, the BRICS have sought to strengthen their military cooperation and hold joint exercises to demonstrate their deterrence capabilities.

It remains to be seen how the military and political leverage of the BRICS will evolve in relation to the dominance of the US dollar. While the BRICS have made progress to strengthen their economic sovereignty and reduce the influence of the dollar, the US dollar remains the dominant reserve currency and remains the currency of choice for international trade. The BRICS countries face challenges such as integrating their national markets, strengthening their institutions and creating a stable and secure economic environment to achieve their goals.

Overall, the BRICS countries have created a dynamic with their military and political leverage over the hegemony of the US dollar that is changing the global balance of power. The rise of China and Russia as major players in the global arena has led to increasing multipolarity in which the BRICS countries play a larger role.

The BRICS countries have created a dynamic with their military and political leverage over the hegemony of the US dollar that is changing the global balance of power. The rise of China and Russia as major players in the global arena has led to increasing multipolarity in which the BRICS countries play a larger role. The effects of this change will be felt for many years to come and will shape the global political and economic landscape.

The security cooperation of the BRICS Countries

The BRICS are a significant alliance on a global level. In addition to economic aspects, these countries have also started to cooperate more closely on security issues. Security cooperation among the BRICS is of great importance as it has the potential to change the geopolitical balance and promote peace and stability in the world. In this chapter, we want to examine in more detail the various aspects and challenges of security cooperation among the BRICS.

In the early years, the cooperation of the BRICS was mainly focused on economic issues. However, over time, member countries realized the need to expand their cooperation to include security issues as well. Security cooperation became an important pillar of BRICS cooperation as member states realized that a stable security situation is crucial for their economic development and regional influence. The BRICS have common interests in issues such as territorial security, military balance vis-à-vis the US, counterterrorism, regional conflicts, cybersecurity and maritime security.

Although BRICS security cooperation has great potential, it also faces some challenges. One of the main problems is the heterogeneity of BRICS countries. They differ in their political systems, priorities and security policy orientations. This can lead to disagreements and obstacles when it comes to formulating and implementing common security strategies. In addition, historical conflicts and territorial disputes between some BRICS members, such as China and Russia, can make cooperation difficult. It is therefore crucial that BRICS countries develop mechanisms to address these challenges and build trust among each other.

BRICS security cooperation takes place at different levels and in different areas. An important platform is the BRICS Summit, where high-level representatives of member states come together to discuss common strategies and policies. In addition, there are also regular meetings of BRICS defense ministers and security officials to promote military cooperation and information sharing. Expert groups have also been established to address specific issues such as counterterrorism, cybersecurity and maritime security.

Despite some challenges, BRICS security cooperation has already achieved some successes. One example is the increased cooperation in the field of counterterrorism. Member states have stepped up their efforts to combat transnational terrorism and are coordinating their actions to combat terrorist threats more effectively. In addition, BRICS have also intensified the exchange of intelligence and best practices in the field of cybersecurity.

In terms of the future prospects of BRICS security cooperation, there is room for further growth and deepening of cooperation. Member states can increase their efforts in conflict prevention and crisis management to promote regional stability. They can also expand their cooperation in the areas of maritime security and critical infrastructure protection. BRICS play an active role in promoting international peace and security by coordinating their positions in international forums such as the United Nations.

But the BRICS countries have also increasingly focused on building up their military capabilities and strengthening their role as a geopolitical force in recent years. Although they do not act as a direct military counterweight to the United States, they can play a significant role in some areas.

The BRICS countries as a whole have considerable military resources. China is the most populous country in the world and has one of the largest armies with modern equipment. It also has a strong navy and air force. Russia, a country with a large arsenal of nuclear weapons, also has a well-equipped army and has advanced its military modernization in recent years. Brazil has a well-equipped army and navy and has taken an active role in peacekeeping missions. India is one of the largest arms exporters and has a sizeable nuclear force. South Africa has a modern army and extensive experience in peacekeeping operations.

The BRICS countries also have the potential to act as a military counterweight to the US due to their regional leverage and geopolitical importance. China is an emerging superpower in Asia and has continuously expanded its influence in the region. It has strategic interests in the South China Sea and has increased its military potential in recent years. Russia is a major player in Eurasia and has shown its presence in conflict zones such as Syria and Ukraine. India plays a crucial role in South Asia and has tensions with Pakistan and China. Brazil has a dominant position in Latin America and is politically and economically influential in the region. South Africa is a major player in Africa and has played a mediating role in regional conflicts in the past.

The BRICS countries have also started to increase their cooperation in military affairs. They hold joint military exercises, conduct regular military-level dialogues and coordinate their positions in international forums. This cooperation aims to build trust among the BRICS countries and explore the possibility of a common security strategy. Although this cooperation is still in its early stages, it has the potential to strengthen the BRICS countries as a collective force in military affairs.

However, there are also challenges and limitations to BRICS security cooperation as a military counterweight to the US. BRICS countries are heterogeneous and have different geopolitical interests and priorities. They also have different military capabilities and resources. This may limit the ability of BRICS countries to present a unified and coordinated military force. In addition, historical conflicts and territorial disputes among some BRICS members may hinder cooperation.

In summary, BRICS countries have the potential to act as a military counterweight to the US. By expanding their military capabilities, exerting regional influence and increasing cooperation in military affairs, BRICS countries can play a greater role in global security issues. However, it is important to note that BRICS security cooperation is still in its early stages and various challenges must be overcome to achieve its full potential as a military counterweight to the US.

Thus, BRICS security cooperation is a dynamic process that has gained importance over time. Member States have recognized that their cooperation on security issues is crucial to protect their national and common interests and promote peace in the world. Despite some challenges, the BRICS countries have already achieved successes and have potential for further progress. By expanding their cooperation in various areas, the BRICS countries can contribute to a stronger and more secure world.

The future of the BRICS Countries and the international financial system

The BRICS countries have undergone impressive economic development in recent years and have grown into important players in the global economy. With their growing influence and economic strength, they are casting a shadow over the international financial system and posing new challenges to the existing order.

The BRICS countries are a group of emerging economies that have a number of similarities. Although they are geographically and culturally diverse, they share a desire for economic growth and political independence. In recent decades, these countries have made significant progress and become major players on the global stage.

The BRICS countries have experienced remarkable economic development in recent years. Their combined GDP now accounts for a significant portion of global economic output. China in particular has undergone rapid development and has risen to become one of the largest economies in the world. This economic strength has given the BRICS countries a greater political voice on the international stage.

The BRICS countries have also increased their cooperation in various areas. They have concluded trade agreements, made investments and sought closer economic integration. They have also pushed for the creation of financial institutions such as the New Development Bank to finance their development projects.

The increasing economic importance of the BRICS countries poses completely new challenges to the international financial system. The previous order, which was dominated by the western industrialized nations, must adapt to meet the new realities. The BRICS countries have a different perspective on economic issues and strive to adequately represent their interests.

One of the challenges is to strengthen the representative voice of the BRICS countries in the existing global financial institutions such as the International Monetary Fund (IMF) and the World Bank. These institutions were established after World War II and do not reflect the current balance of power. The BRICS countries are pushing for a reform of these institutions to adequately take their voices into account.

Another challenge is to create alternatives to the established international financial system. The BRICS countries have taken a first step in this direction with the establishment of the New Development Bank. This bank aims to finance infrastructure and development projects in the BRICS and other developing countries. Through such initiatives, the BRICS are trying to reduce their dependence on the established financial institutions, gain greater autonomy and influence.

The BRICS countries have promising future prospects. Their economic growth is expected to continue to exceed the global average. They have a young and growing population that offers enormous potential for the domestic market and workforce. Their rich natural resources and technological capabilities are valuable resources that will help them advance their development.

In addition, the BRICS countries are expected to further deepen their cooperation in the coming years. They will find new ways to expand trade relations and encourage investment. They will also consider creating new financial institutions and instruments to better represent their interests and strengthen their economic sovereignty.

However, the future of the BRICS countries in the international financial system is fraught with uncertainty. It is unclear how quickly and to what extent they will achieve their goals. They will also face challenges such as political differences, geopolitical tensions and economic volatility. Nevertheless, their influence on the global economy and the international financial system remains an important development that should be carefully monitored.

To meet the challenges posed by the BRICS countries, several reforms in the international financial system have been discussed in recent years. One of the most important discussions revolves around the representative voice of the BRICS countries in the global financial institutions. The BRICS countries demand greater participation and say in decisions that affect their interests.

One area that is particularly controversial is the role of the World Bank and the International Monetary Fund (IMF). These institutions were founded by the western industrialized countries after World War II and have come to occupy a dominant position in the global financial architecture. The BRICS countries argue that the world has changed fundamentally since then and that the composition and decision-making processes of these institutions must be adapted to current developments.

To meet these demands, various reform proposals have been made. One option is to increase the voting rights of the BRICS countries in the existing institutions. This would ensure that their interests are adequately taken into account. Another approach is to create new institutions specifically tailored to the needs of the BRICS countries. The establishment of the New Development Bank was a first step in this direction, but further initiatives may follow.

Another aspect of the reform discussion concerns the creation of an alternative reserve currency system. Currently, the US dollar dominates as the international reserve currency, which the BRICS countries feel is unfair. They have suggested that the International Monetary Fund could introduce a new reserve currency that is not tied to a single nation, but this idea has not yet been implemented and remains the subject of further discussion.

The growing importance of the BRICS countries in the international financial system also has geopolitical implications. The traditional dominance of the western industrialized nations is increasingly being challenged, and a multipolar world order is emerging. The BRICS countries have raised their voices in political affairs and are looking for ways to represent their interests on a global level.

The BRICS countries are also seeking to expand their regional spheres of influence. China has launched the Belt and Road Initiative (BRI), an ambitious infrastructure project designed to promote trade and cooperation with countries along the Eurasian landmass. Russia is seeking closer integration with the countries of the former Soviet Union and has taken a leading role in the Eurasian Economic Union.

These geopolitical shifts towards the east are affecting existing power structures and alliances. The BRICS countries are looking for new partners and collaborations to strengthen their interests. They are also establishing close relationships with other emerging economies and developing countries to amplify their voice on a global level.

Despite their impressive growth and increasing importance, the BRICS also face challenges and risks. One of the biggest risks is economic volatility. The BRICS are closely linked to the global economy and therefore external shocks and crises can affect their growth prospects. A slowdown in global demand, a rise in commodity prices or trade conflicts can have a negative impact on the BRICS.

Another risk is political and geopolitical tensions. The BRICS have different political systems and interests, which can lead to conflicts. Geopolitical tensions, territorial disputes and protectionist measures can hinder cooperation and integration among the BRICS.

In addition, the BRICS face sustainable development and environmental challenges. Their growth has led to pollution, resource scarcity and social inequalities. The BRICS need to rethink their development strategies and pursue more sustainable models to ensure long-term growth and prosperity.

The future of the BRICS countries in the international financial system depends on the successful implementtation of reforms, overcoming challenges and risks, and cooperating with other nations and regional organizations. The BRICS countries face the challenge of advancing their development in a sustainable manner while protecting their national interests.

The coming years will show how the BRICS countries will develop and what role they will play in the international financial system. Their economic strength and growing influence will undoubtedly shape the global economic and financial architecture. It remains to be seen how well they will be able to represent their interests and find common solutions to global challenges.

They have grown into important players in the global economy and have the potential to change the international financial system for the long term. Their economic strength and increasing cooperation pose new challenges to the existing order.

All in all, the BRICS countries have become an increasing counterweight to the Western financial system in recent years. The BRICS countries have undergone impressive economic development and have grown into major economies. Together they represent a significant share of global economic output and have a significant volume of trade with each other. Their combined markets offer enormous opportunities for international investors and companies. This economic strength makes the BRICS countries attractive partners and creates a counterforce to the dominant Western financial system.

The political influence of the BRICS countries has also increased. They have raised their voices in international forums such as the United Nations, the G20 and the WTO and are trying to adequately represent their interests. Through their cooperation and joint positioning in global affairs, they have gained greater political capacity to act.

This strengthens their profile as a counterweight to the Western financial system and enables them to put forward alternative proposals and perspectives.

A central point of the BRICS countries is their call for reform of the international financial system.

They argue that existing institutions such as the International Monetary Fund (IMF) and the World Bank no longer reflect today's realities and must adequately take into account the interests of emerging economies. The BRICS countries are demanding a greater representative voice and a more balanced decision-making process. They have also created their own institutions such as the New Development Bank to finance their development projects and strengthen their autonomy. These reform efforts are an important step in changing the Western financial system towards a fairer and more balanced order.

The importance of the BRICS countries as a counterweight to the Western financial system lies in their ability to offer alternative perspectives and solutions. Through their economic strength and political influence, they can challenge existing power structures and dominance. This promotes competition, strengthens the diversity of approaches and creates a more balanced global financial system.

It is important to note that the BRICS countries are not trying to replace the Western financial system. Rather, they are striving for a fairer and more balanced global financial architecture that adequately takes into account their interests. Through their cooperation and dialogue with the Western financial system, they can contribute to constructive change and develop a new form of coexistence and cooperation.

Overall, the BRICS countries provide an important counterweight to the Western financial system. Their economic strength, political influence and reform efforts have helped to make the international financial system more diverse and resilient. The importance of the BRICS countries as a counterweight is expected to continue to grow as they deepen their cooperation and represent their interests more effectively at the global level.

The growing conflict between the BRICS countries and the Western financial system is reflected in various areas. While the BRICS countries raise their voices and pursue alternative approaches, there is often skepticism and resistance to the demands of the BRICS countries on the part of the "old force". This conflict has implications for the global financial architecture and cooperation between actors.

A key point of contention between the BRICS and the Western financial system is the question of institutional reforms. The BRICS are calling for fairer representation and a more balanced decision-making process in existing institutions such as the IMF and the World Bank. They argue that these institutions do not reflect the current balance of power and do not adequately consider the voices of emerging economies. On the other hand, there is often resistance in the Western financial system to a redistribution of power and resources, as this would challenge the existing hierarchy.

Another area of conflict concerns the issue of reserve currencies. The US dollar currently dominates as an international reserve currency, which is perceived as unfair by the BRICS. They are calling for the creation of an alternative reserve currency that is not tied to a single nation. However, this proposal has been received with skepticism by the Western financial system, as such a change could have a significant impact on the stability and value of reserve currencies.

The conflict between the BRICS and the Western financial system also extends to the area of trade and investment. The BRICS have increased their cooperation in these areas and concluded regional trade agreements. They have also expanded their investments in infrastructure projects and strategic industries. These developments are often viewed with suspicion and perceived as a threat to established trade patterns and investment flows.

The growing conflict between the BRICS and the Western financial system has also taken on geopolitical dimensions. The BRICS are looking for alternative partners and alliances to strengthen their interests. This can lead to tensions with established powers and existing alliances. Geopolitical conflicts and rival interests can hinder the BRICS' cooperation and integration with the Western financial system.

The increasing tensions between the BRICS and the Western financial system are posing challenges to the global financial architecture. Existing power structures are being challenged and a multipolar world order is emerging. While the BRICS countries pursue alternative approaches and strive for a fairer and more balanced order, there are often reservations and concerns on the part of the

Western financial system about the consequences of such changes.

It is important to note that the conflict between the BRICS countries and the Western financial system does not necessarily have to lead to a complete split. There is still room for dialogue, negotiation and compromise. Both sides have an interest in a stable and fair global financial architecture. The challenge is to find ways to recognize the legitimate interests and concerns of all actors and to find solutions that are both fair and workable.

The growing conflict between the BRICS countries and the Western financial system is a complex and multifaceted issue. It requires comprehensive analysis and constructive dialogue to find possible ways to overcome differences and create a cooperative and balanced global financial architecture.

The BRICS have legitimate concerns about a fairer and more balanced global financial architecture. They are calling for a greater representative voice in existing institutions such as the IMF and the World Bank and the creation of alternative reserve currencies. Their economic strength and efforts at regional cooperation have led to increased integration and increasing influence in the global economy.

On the other hand, there are often reservations and concerns about such changes within the Western financial system. The existing hierarchy and distribution of power are being questioned, and there are concerns about instability and uncertainty. The conflict between the BRICS and the Western financial system poses challenges to the global financial architecture and requires comprehensive analysis and constructive dialogue.

The future of the BRICS in the international financial system remains uncertain and depends on various factors, including the implementation of reforms, the management of challenges and risks, and the willingness to cooperate and engage in dialogue. The BRICS have the potential to transform the international financial system and create a fairer order, but further efforts and negotiations are needed to find a constructive way forward.

Overall, the BRICS countries represent an important counterforce to the Western financial system. Their economic strength, political influence and reform efforts have set the global financial architecture in motion. The growing conflict between the BRICS countries and the Western financial system opens up the opportunity for a redesign of the global financial order that is fairer and more balanced. It is the responsibility of all actors to find solutions together to create a sustainable and inclusive global financial architecture that meets the needs and interests of all.

The US reaction to the BRICS Countries

In recent decades, the BRICS countries have emerged as major global players. With their emerging economies and growing political influences, the BRICS countries have brought a new dynamic to the international arena. This change in the geopolitical landscape has also forced the US to adapt its strategies and respond appropriately to the growing power of the BRICS countries.

The US response to the BRICS countries has been multifaceted and reflected in various areas, including economics, diplomacy, and security. The US viewed the BRICS countries as challenges because they have the potential to influence the existing world order and challenge US dominance.

On an economic level, the US is responding to the growing economic power of the BRICS countries by building increased trade relations with these countries. The US recognizes the enormous market potential of the BRICS countries and strives to promote economic partnerships and investment opportunities. By expanding trade with the BRICS countries, the US is trying to boost its own economy and secure its position as a leading economic power.

At the same time, however, the US is also trying to curb the growing competition from the BRICS countries, especially in the fields of technology and innovation. The US is investing more in research and development to maintain its technological superiority and outperform the BRICS countries in this field. It took measures to protect intellectual property and limit the BRICS countries' access to Western technology. This strategy aims to slow down the BRICS countries' technological development and maintain dependence on the US as a leading technology supplier.

In the diplomatic field, the US is trying to strengthen its relations with the BRICS countries and influence their political decisions. It organizes regular summits and bilateral talks to intensify dialogue with the BRICS countries and identify common interests. At the same time, the US is trying to convince the BRICS countries to adhere to existing international norms and institutions and to align their political actions with the US's ideas of global stability and democracy.

On the security front, the US is responding to the BRICS by increasing its military presence and security cooperation in strategically important regions. It sees the growing military power of some BRICS countries as a potential threat to its own interests and seeks to maintain its dominance in critical regions such as the Middle East, the South Pacific and Africa. The US is increasing its cooperation with regional allies and increasing its military presence to counter potential threats from the BRICS countries.

It is important to note that the US response to the BRICS countries has not been uniform and has been influenced by different political actors and interest groups. There have been voices advocating constructive cooperation with the BRICS countries and trying to create synergies between the US and the BRICS countries. Others, on the other hand, have seen the BRICS countries as rivals and threats and are calling for a tougher approach towards them.

The US response to the BRICS is a complex process shaped by various factors such as geopolitical considerations, economic interests and security concerns. The US seeks to maintain its own position as a leading global superpower while responding to the challenges and opportunities presented by the rise of the BRICS. This response has evolved over time and has been characterized by ongoing adaptation to the changing geopolitical reality.

The US response to the BRICS continues at the political level. The US certainly recognizes the growing importance of the BRICS countries as political actors and seeks to strengthen its relations with them, both bilaterally and through closer cooperation in international organizations such as the United Nations, the World Bank and the International Monetary Fund.

The US uses its diplomatic channels to align its positions and interests with the BRICS countries and to find common solutions to global challenges. However, there are also tensions and disagreements on both sides, for example on issues such as human rights, democracy and regional conflicts.

One area in which the US is particularly responsive to the BRICS is the issue of global governance. The US has traditionally played a strong role in shaping the international order, and the rise of the BRICS countries has been seen by some as a challenge to that system. The US is trying to integrate the BRICS countries into existing international institutions and encourage them to abide by the global rules of the game that have been defined so far. At the same time, however, there has also been discussion about reforming and adapting these institutions to reflect the changing balance of power in the world.

The US is increasingly aware that a purely confrontational attitude towards the BRICS countries is not productive. It is gradually realizing the benefits of cooperation and constructive dialogue to address common challenges, such as climate change, international terrorism or the stability of global financial markets. In some areas, the US has therefore worked with the BRICS countries to find solutions that meet both its own interests and those of the BRICS countries.

For example, the US is seeking to engage the BRICS in international climate negotiations and encourage them to set and implement their own emissions targets. By sharing technologies and expertise and promoting investments in renewable energy, the US is seeking to find common ground with the BRICS and take joint steps to reduce greenhouse gas emissions.

Overall, the US response to the BRICS is characterized by a mix of cooperation and competition. The US recognizes the opportunities and challenges presented by the rise of the BRICS and seeks to maintain its own position as a global superpower. It uses diplomatic, economic, and security tools to deal with the BRICS and defend its own interests.

It is important to note that the US response to the BRICS has evolved and adapted over time. The dynamic between the US and the BRICS is characterized by interactions, tensions, and cooperation. The US, on the one hand, is seeking a balance between protecting its own interests and recognizing the new geopolitical reality brought by the

BRICS countries, while on the other hand, it is trying to undermine the influence of the BRICS countries in order to preserve the dominance of the US dollar.

The US reaction to the BRICS countries continues at the political level. The US recognizes the growing importance of the BRICS countries as political actors and seeks to strengthen its relations with them. This is done both bilaterally and through cooperation in international organizations such as the United Nations, the World Bank and the International Monetary Fund.

The US uses its diplomatic channels to coordinate its positions and interests with the BRICS countries, but there are also tensions and disagreements, particularly on issues such as NATO expansion and influencing decisions made by EU states.

One area in which the US has been particularly responsive to the BRICS countries has been the issue of global governance. The US has traditionally played a strong role in shaping the international order, and the rise of the BRICS countries has been seen by some as a challenge to that system. At the same time, however, there has also been discussion about reforms and adapting these institutions to reflect the changing balance of power in the world.

Another important dimension of the US response to the BRICS countries is public diplomacy. The US recognizes the importance of public opinion regarding the BRICS countries and strives to promote a positive perception of the US. This is done through cultural exchanges, educational programs and expanding media presence in the BRICS countries.

Overall, the US response to the BRICS has been characterized by a mix of cooperation and competition. The US recognizes the threats and challenges to its hegemony posed by the rise of the BRICS and seeks to preserve its own position as a global superpower. It uses diplomatic, economic and security tools to deal with the BRICS and defend its own interests.

It is important to note that the US response to the BRICS will need to evolve and adapt over time. The dynamic between the US and the BRICS is one of interaction, tension and cooperation. The US seeks a balance between safeguarding its own interests and recognizing the new geopolitical reality brought by the BRICS.

The BRICS Countries and regional integration

The BRICS countries have witnessed remarkable development in recent years. These emerging economies have joined forces to promote their common interests and advance their regional integration. In this chapter, we will take an in-depth look at the BRICS countries and their contribution to regional integration.

A key aspect of the BRICS countries' regional integration lies in their economic cooperation. These countries have realized that by expanding their trade relations and encouraging investment, they can strengthen their collective economic strength. In 2010, the BRICS Interbank Cooperation was introduced to promote cooperation in the financial sector. In addition, the BRICS countries have taken initiatives to facilitate trade and investment among member countries.

Apart from economic cooperation, political cooperation and security also play an important role in the BRICS countries' regional integration. These countries have held regular summits to discuss their common positions and formulate policies. They have also united their voices at the international level to represent their interests and promote a multipolar world order.

Promoting cultural exchange and education is another important aspect of BRICS regional integration. Countries have established programs to promote cultural exchange, such as student and artist exchange programs. By sharing ideas, knowledge, and cultural practices, BRICS have helped strengthen understanding and solidarity among member countries.

Although BRICS have made progress in their regional integration, they also face various challenges. Some of the challenges include different political systems, economic differences, cultural differences, and language barriers. Nevertheless, BRICS also offer great opportunities for their regional integration. By working together, they can leverage their individual strengths and find common solutions to global challenges.

An important aspect of BRICS regional integration lies in developing infrastructure projects and promoting regional connectivity. These countries have realized that well-developed infrastructure and improved connectivity are crucial to facilitate trade, investment and exchange of goods and services. Therefore, the BRICS countries have taken various initiatives to promote the development of roads, railways, ports and telecommunication networks. These projects contribute to the economic development and integration of the region.

Another important aspect of the BRICS regional integration is environmental protection and the promotion of sustainable development. In view of the growing environmental problems, such as climate change, water scarcity and pollution, the BRICS countries have realized that they need to work together to address these challenges. They have taken initiatives to promote renewable energy, protect biodiversity and reduce greenhouse gas emissions. By taking a joint approach, the BRICS countries can bring about positive changes at the global level and promote sustainable development.

The BRICS regional integration also includes the social aspect and cultural exchange. These countries have developed programs to promote social integration and cultural exchange to strengthen understanding and connection between people. By sharing cultural practices, traditions, art and music, BRICS countries can celebrate the diversity and richness of their cultures while promoting harmony and dialogue.

Another important area of regional integration of BRICS countries is education and knowledge exchange. These countries have recognized that quality education and the exchange of knowledge and innovations are crucial to drive economic development and social progress. Therefore, BRICS countries have established programs to promote educational exchange, research cooperation and technology transfer. This allows member countries to learn from each other, improve their education system and develop innovative solutions to common challenges.

The BRICS have already made significant progress in their regional integration, but challenges and opportunities also remain for the future. One of the challenges is to achieve balanced development among member countries as they have different sizes, resources and levels of development. It is important that the BRICS continue to develop common goals and strategies to ensure that no one is left behind. In addition, they must also respond to global changes, such as the rise of new technologies, demographic changes and geopolitical shifts.

The BRICS have become an influential force in the global arena and have advanced their regional integration. Through economic cooperation, political cooperation, cultural exchanges, infrastructure projects and other initiatives, they have strengthened their ties and promoted their common interests. Although challenges exist, the BRICS also offer great opportunities for sustainable development, social integration and economic strength. By deepening their cooperation and pooling their resources, the BRICS can play a significant role in shaping the global agenda and creating a more equitable and prosperous world.

In recent years, they have made significant progress in their regional integration. Through their economic cooperation, political collaboration, cultural exchanges and educational programs, they have strengthened their ties and promoted their common interests. Although challenges remain, the BRICS countries are well positioned to advance their regional integration and strengthen their collective voice at the international level.

The BRICS Countries and sustainable development

The BRICS countries have experienced remarkable economic development in recent decades. These emerging economies have not only driven their own growth but also contributed to greater global economic diversity. However, given the size and influence of these countries, it is also crucial that they drive their development in a sustainable manner.

Promoting sustainable development is a key aspect for the BRICS countries. Each of these countries has its own unique challenges and priorities in terms of environmental protection, social justice and economic stability. Nevertheless, they also share common goals and principles to promote sustainable development and combat climate change.

An important aspect of sustainable development for the BRICS countries is protecting natural resources. Brazil, for example, has one of the world's most important green lungs, the Amazon rainforest. It is crucial that Brazil and the other BRICS countries take action to reduce deforestation, protect biodiversity and promote the sustainable use of natural resources. This requires close cooperation at national and international level, as well as investments in sustainable agriculture, renewable energy and ecosystem protection.

Another key element of sustainable development is promoting a fair and inclusive society. India, for example, faces the challenge of tackling poverty and improving access to education, healthcare and basic services. BRICS countries must join forces to ensure that no one in their population is left behind and that social inequalities are reduced. This requires investments in social infrastructure, strengthening education systems and creating opportunities for disadvantaged populations.

In addition, BRICS countries play an important role in promoting renewable energy and combating climate change. China has made great strides in the development and implementation of solar energy and wind power in recent years. These technologies are not only environmentally friendly, but also create jobs and promote economic development. BRICS countries should increase their efforts in renewable energy research and development and promote the exchange of best practices and technologies to accelerate the transition to a sustainable energy supply.

It is also important that the BRICS countries are involved in international climate agreements and arrangements. Russia, Brazil and China are among the largest emitters of greenhouse gases in the world. India and South Africa are also significant players. To effectively address climate change, these countries must reduce their emissions and commit to green and sustainable development. This requires cooperation with other countries and support for climate change adaptation and emission reduction initiatives.

The BRICS countries have the potential to take a leading role in promoting sustainable development worldwide. By aligning their own national priorities with global goals, they can develop innovative solutions to the most pressing challenges of our time. This includes promoting sustainable business practices, investing in green technologies and creating an enabling environment for sustainable growth.

The BRICS countries are aware that sustainable development not only includes environmental and social aspects, but also offers economic opportunities. By promoting green investments and sustainable business models, they can strengthen their competitiveness and open up new markets. At the same time, they should ensure that the benefits of economic growth are shared fairly and no one is excluded.

The BRICS countries have already made some progress in promoting sustainable development, but there is still much to be done. It requires a long-term commitment and close cooperation among countries to achieve the Sustainable Development Goals. By sharing experiences, building capacities and implementing projects together, the BRICS countries can create a sustainable future for themselves and for the world.

The BRICS countries face challenges, but they also have the opportunity to be a transformative force for sustainable development. By pooling their resources, knowledge and innovations, they can not only promote their own growth but also create a sustainable, equitable and inclusive world for all. The future is in their hands and the world is looking forward to seeing how the BRICS countries will tackle the challenges of sustainable development and create a sustainable future.

The BRICS countries have not only made economic progress but have also taken impressive steps in terms of sustainable political development. Each country has its own specific challenges and progress in this area, but they also share common characteristics and aspirations to promote political stability, participation and good governance.

Brazil, the largest country in Latin America, has experienced significant changes in its political landscape in recent decades. It has evolved from a long period of authoritarian regimes to a democratic government. Although challenges still exist, particularly in terms of corruption and inequality, Brazil has made progress to strengthen political institutions, promote the separation of powers, and protect citizens' rights. In addition, in recent years Brazil has taken initiatives to promote civil society participation and strengthen civic education to increase awareness of democratic processes and the importance of political participation.

Russia has also undergone an interesting political evolution. After the collapse of the Soviet Union, the country experienced a period of political upheaval and uncertainty. However, in recent years, Russia has taken steps to strengthen its political institutions and promote political stability. It has implemented reforms to improve the balance of power between the executive, legislative and judicial branches and to strengthen the rule of law. At the same time, concerns about political freedoms, press freedom and human rights in Russia remain. Finding a proper balance between political stability and individual freedoms remains a challenge.

India, the world's largest democratic nation, has a long tradition of political participation and public engagement. Political development in India has been marked by steady progress towards a pluralistic democracy in which various political parties and interest groups play an active role. India has also made progress in promoting political rights and strengthening citizen participation. However, challenges remain regarding corruption, inefficient bureaucracy and regional conflicts affecting the political system. India needs to continue its efforts to strengthen political institutions, promote transparency and accountability, and address social and economic inequalities.

China, the world's most populous country, has a unique political structure characterized by one-party communist rule. Although there are restrictions on political freedoms and freedom of expression, China has nevertheless made impressive progress in terms of economic development and poverty alleviation. The political system in China is characterized by strong central leadership aimed at stability and economic growth. In recent years, China has also taken measures to strengthen the rule of law and encourage citizen participation at the local level. However, achieving a balance between political control and political participation remains a challenge.

South Africa, the only African country in the BRICS group, has undergone an impressive political transformation after the end of apartheid. South Africa has one of the most progressive constitutions in the world that protects political rights and individual freedoms. It has also built strong political institutions and developed a pluralistic political process. However, South Africa faces challenges related to corruption, social inequality and persistent economic disparities. It requires continued efforts to promote more equitable and inclusive political development and ensure political participation of all citizens.

Overall, the BRICS countries have made considerable efforts to promote political stability, participation and good governance. Each country has its own challenges and there is room for further improvement. The BRICS countries can learn from each other and share best practices to strengthen their political development and shape a sustainable future. By promoting political participation, protecting human rights and strengthening political institutions, the BRICS countries can help build stable and equitable societies that lay the foundation for sustainable development.

The BRICS countries have pursued ambitious expansion plans in recent years to increase their presence and influence both in their own regions and at the global level. Each country has specific strategies and priorities for their expansion, but they also share common goals and aspirations to expand their economic and political power.

Brazil, as one of the largest countries in South America, has focused on strengthening its presence in the region and expanding its economic ties with Latin American countries. Brazil has taken an active role in promoting regional integration and cooperation through initiatives such as MERCOSUR (Common Market of the South). In addition, Brazil has also increased its engagement in other emerging markets, particularly in Africa. It has invested in infrastructure projects and signed trade agreements to expand its economic presence and access to raw materials.

Russia, as the world's largest country by area, has focused its expansion plans on various areas. It has pushed ahead with the expansion of its military presence in some regions and expanded its sphere of influence. Russia has also strengthened its political and economic relations with Eurasian countries by establishing the Eurasian Economic Union. This union aims to promote trade, economic integration and cooperation among member countries. In addition, Russia has used its energy resources to expand its sphere of influence in Europe and establish energy partnerships with various countries.

India, as an emerging economic power and the most populous country in the world, has expanded its expansion plans to various areas. India has increased its engagement in the South Asian region and supported initiatives such as the SAARC (South Asian Association for Regional Cooperation) to promote economic cooperation and integration in the region. In addition, India has also taken an active role in multilateral forums such as the United Nations to strengthen its voice in global affairs. India has also intensified its economic ties with African countries to expand its access to raw materials and markets.

China, as the second largest economy in the world, has pursued extensive expansion both in the Asia-Pacific region and globally. China has pushed ahead with building close economic ties with many countries and regions in Asia and has become one of the largest trading partners of many countries. China has also made massive investments in infrastructure projects such as the Belt and Road Initiative (BRI) to strengthen its ties with countries in Asia, Europe, Africa and the Middle East. The BRI aims to promote trade, investment and economic integration along historic trade routes and expand the Chinese sphere of influence.

South Africa, the only African country in the BRICS group, has extended its expansion plans to the African continent. South Africa has focused on strengthening its role as a regional player and promoting economic integration in Africa. It has supported initiatives such as the African Union and sought to reduce trade barriers and facilitate cross-border trade. In addition, South Africa has also increased its diplomatic efforts to expand its political presence and influence on the African continent.

The BRICS countries have recognized that their expansion brings both opportunities and challenges. While pursuing their economic and political interests, they must also ensure that their expansion is carried out in a sustainable and responsible manner. They must ensure that their activities are consistent with the principles of global governance, sustainable development and respect for the sovereignty of other countries.

The BRICS' expansion plans reflect their desire to play a more active role in the global economy and world politics. Through their growing economic and political power, the BRICS can help address global problems and promote a multipolar world order. It is important that they shape their expansion in a way that takes into account the interests of other countries and regions and helps promote peace, stability and sustainable development.

The BRICS' expansion plans not only impact their own region, but also the global balance of power and the interests of other actors, especially the United States. The United States has a strong interest in maintaining its dominant position in the global economy and world politics. Therefore, they see the growing economic and political power of the BRICS as a potential challenge and have conflicting interests regarding their expansion.

One area where the interests of the United States and the BRICS clash is economic competition. The BRICS, particularly China, have experienced impressive economic development in recent years and have become major players in the global economy. This has led to increased competition with the US, particularly in terms of trade, investment and market access. The US sees the economic expansion of the BRICS as a threat to its own economic interests and seeks to take measures to limit competition and preserve its economic dominance.

Another area where there are opposing interests is geopolitical influence. The BRICS, particularly Russia and China, have expanded their political and military presence in various regions. This has led to tensions with the US as they see their dominant position in certain regions and their strategic interests threatened. There are conflicts and rivalries, particularly in regions such as the Middle East, the South China Sea and Eastern Europe, where US and BRICS interests clash.

In addition, there are also different views and interests regarding global governance and multilateral institutions. The BRICS countries have increased their voice and influence in international forums such as the United Nations, the World Trade Organization and other multilateral organizations in recent years. They seek greater representation and a fairer global order. The US, on the other hand, has traditionally been interested in a world order centered around it and has played a leading role in shaping and enforcing global rules and institutions. The different views and interests regarding global governance have led to tensions and conflicts between the US and the BRICS countries.

It is important to note that the interests of the US and the BRICS countries are not necessarily completely opposed. There are areas where cooperation and coordination are possible, such as tackling global challenges such as climate change, counterterrorism and securing the global trading system. Nevertheless, the opposing interests remain in many areas and require skillful diplomacy and willingness to negotiate to avoid conflict and find common solutions.

The relationship between the USA and the BRICS countries is complex and influenced by many factors. The expansion plans of the BRICS countries pose a challenge to the dominant position of the USA and lead to conflicts and tensions in various areas. Constructive cooperation requires dialogue, mutual recognition of interests and the search for compromises. Only through a balanced and cooperative approach can the USA and the BRICS countries successfully pursue their interests on a global level and contribute to promoting stability and sustainable development.

The BRICS Countries and the Mercosur Alliance

The BRICS and Mercosur are two major economic and political alliances that, with the exception of Brazil, operate on different continents and yet pursue common goals and interests - international trade without the US dollar. Here we will look at the background, history, goals and commonalities of these two alliances in order to gain a comprehensive understanding of their relationship with the US dollar.

The idea of forming the BRICS into a close partnership, as we know, arose in response to the increasing economic dominance of the western industrialized countries, especially the G7 countries. The BRICS aimed to strengthen their voice in international economic issues and promote the creation of a multipolar world order. The BRICS, as we have already discussed in detail, have a number of common goals and interests that drive their cooperation.

The Mercado Común del Sur (Mercosur), in English "Common Market of the South", is an economic alliance of South American countries that aims to promote economic integration and political cooperation. Mercosur was founded in 1991 with the signing of the Asunción Treaty by the founding members Argentina, Brazil, Paraguay and Uruguay.

The idea of creating the Mercosur alliance arose against the backdrop of economic instability in South America in the 1980s. The founding members recognized the need for increased cooperation to reduce trade barriers, promote economic growth and advance regional integration. The Asunción Treaty, which sealed the founding of the Mercosur union, laid the foundations for economic integration between the member countries. This included the reduction of tariffs, the creation of a customs union, the harmonization of trade policies and the promotion of the free movement of goods within the region. Mercosur has grown steadily over the years, and Venezuela joined the alliance as its fifth full member in 2012. However, the country was suspended from the alliance in 2016 for violating democratic principles. Mercosur currently consists of four full members: Argentina, Brazil, Paraguay and Uruguay.

Mercosur has similar goals to the BRICS countries when it comes to economic integration and political cooperation.

Reducing trade barriers and creating a common market are key concerns of Mercosur. These include tariff-free trade for the majority of goods, eliminating non-tariff barriers to trade and harmonizing trade rules.

Mercosur aims to promote the economic development of its member countries through increased cooperation and the expansion of regional value chains.

In addition to economic aspects, Mercosur also aims to achieve closer political cooperation between members in order to address common challenges and represent a unified position in international affairs.

Mercosur also promotes the exchange of cultural goods and services and promotes social integration in the region.

Despite its ambitions and successes, the Mercosur alliance also faces some challenges.

Mercosur member countries have different economic, political and social structures. This sometimes leads to disagreements and tensions, especially with regard to trade policy and market access.

The question of how Mercosur should shape its relations with other regions and economic powers is a challenge. The alliance partners have different strategic priorities and interests when it comes to negotiating trade agreements with third countries.

As with many international organizations, Mercosur also has concerns about democratic legitimacy and accountability. Some member countries criticize that decisions in the organization are made undemocratically and that their sovereignty is compromised. But external factors such as global economic crises or geopolitical tensions can also have a negative impact on economic stability and trade relations within Mercosur.

BRICS and Mercosur - similarities and differences

Despite their geographical separation and different memberships, BRICS and Mercosur have some similarities.

Both the BRICS and Mercosur member countries play important roles in the global economy. They have signify-cant resources and large populations, giving them a strong negotiating position in international affairs.

The BRICS and Mercosur seek sovereignty and equality in the international arena. They see the need for a multipolar world order in which their voices are heard and respected.

Both alliances are committed to reducing trade barriers and promoting free trade. They recognize the importance of open markets for economic growth and development.

Despite these similarities, there are also important differ-rences between the two alliances.

While BRICS, with the exception of Brazil, includes mostly Asian and African states, Mercosur is a purely South American alliance.

BRICS has five members with different political and economic structures, while Mercosur currently includes four South American countries with similar regional orientations.

Although both alliances aim at economic cooperation and political coordination, they have quite different focuses and priorities regarding their trade relations and their role in global politics.

Both BRICS and Mercosur face challenges that may affect their effectiveness and their ability to achieve their goals. Some of the challenges they face have been mentioned previously.

Mercosur member countries, particularly Brazil and Argentina, have historically had a heavy dependence on the US dollar in their economic relations. The dollar is often used for trade with third countries outside Mercosur, and member countries' currencies are often pegged to the dollar. In addition, many companies in the region have dollar-denominated debt, making them vulnerable to exchange rate fluctuations.

If Mercosur states were to abandon the US dollar or reduce their dependence, several threats to the dollar and the global economy could arise.

If Mercosur countries, like the BRICS, decide to diversify their foreign exchange reserves and hold fewer dollars, this could lead to a further decline in demand for US dollars. Since they have been major players in demand for dollars so far, this could have an impact on the value of the US currency.

If Mercosur countries were to reduce the use of the dollar in trade with third countries, this could reduce the volume of trade in dollars. The dollar would then lose importance in this regard and other currencies could gain importance.

A decline in demand for the US dollar could affect the value of the dollar relative to other currencies. This could lead to exchange rate fluctuations, which in turn would have an impact on global financial markets and international trade dynamics.

Mercosur countries are currently major buyers of US Treasury bonds, which play a crucial role in financing US debt. If they reduce or stop their bond purchases, this could weigh on US debt markets and affect interest rates in the US.

A gradual diversification of foreign exchange reserves through a wider range of currencies could help to minimise the risk of exchange rate fluctuations and promote the stability of their own currencies.

The Mercosur states can strengthen their cooperation in trade and monetary policy within the alliance. By promoting trade in their own currencies, they would reduce their dependence on the dollar and improve economic integration in the region.

The member countries can conclude strategic trade agreements with other emerging economic powers such as the BRICS countries or other South American countries to facilitate trade in regional currencies and strengthen their economic relations.

A coherent and sustainable monetary policy would help the Mercosur states to strengthen their currencies and minimise the impact of exchange rate fluctuations.

The participation of Mercosur in the BRICS summit in 2023 is an important aspect of the regional and global cooperation between the two alliances. Although Mercosur, with the exception of Brazil, is not a full member of the BRICS, it has been invited as a guest in the past to exchange views and interests and promote closer cooperation.

The BRICS countries have the potential and vision to expand their cooperation beyond their borders and to cooperate with other emerging economies.

The BRICS countries have the potential and vision to expand their cooperation beyond their borders and to connect with other emerging economic powers and regional alliances. Mercosur, as one of the most important regional alliances in South America, was invited to the BRICS summit due to its economic and political importance.

The invitation from Mercosur allows the BRICS to strengthen their reach and influence in the South American region and to build a deeper connection with the Mercosur countries. At the same time, it provides Mercosur with an opportunity to raise its concerns, goals and priorities and to discuss potential partnerships with the BRICS countries.

Participation in the BRICS Summit offers Mercosur several potential benefits and opportunities.

By sharing experiences and best practices with the BRICS countries, the Mercosur countries could gain valuable insights and strengthen their economic cooperation. This would promote trade and investment between the regions.

Participation in the BRICS Summit allows Mercosur to strengthen its role as a regional player and consolidate its position as a major economic and political alliance in South America.

The BRICS countries share similar goals in terms of reforming global governance and promoting a multipolar world order. Participation in the Summit provides

Mercosur with an opportunity to join these aspirations and present a unified position in international affairs.

As the BRICS alliance also seeks to reduce the dominance of the US dollar and increase the use of regional currencies, cooperation with the BRICS countries could help Mercosur reduce its dependence on the dollar and promote currency diversification.

Overall, Mercosur's participation in the BRICS summit presents both opportunities and challenges. It is up to the countries involved to use this opportunity to strengthen their economic cooperation, promote political coordination and unite their voices in the global arena. Close cooperation between the BRICS countries and Mercosur could lead to increased integration and a stronger positioning of the South American region in the global economy and politics.

The US countermeasures against Mercosur-BRICS cooperation may stem from its view that closer cooperation between the South American countries and the emerging BRICS countries would challenge their geopolitical and economic dominance in the region and globally. The US has historically had a strong presence and interests in Latin America and seeks to defend its position through various measures.

The US attempts to engage in diplomatic efforts to disrupt or weaken relations between the BRICS and Mercosur. This is done by exerting pressure on individual Mercosur member countries or by offering economic incentives or development aid to dissuade these countries from working closely with the BRICS.

The US imposes economic sanctions on certain Mercosur member countries to deter them from working with the BRICS. Such sanctions affect trade, investment or financial transactions and aim to foment economic instability in the region and make economic cooperation between Mercosur and BRICS more difficult.

The US continues to attempt to interfere in the internal affairs of Mercosur countries to undermine the political stability and unity of the alliance partners. This is done through targeted propaganda, support for opposition groups or even covert operations to foment political tensions and conflicts.

The US is trying to undermine the legitimacy of Mercosur-BRICS cooperation through lobbying and influencing international organizations and institutions. This may lead to questions being raised about international partnerships and agreements already concluded between the alliances and raise doubts about their effectiveness and usefulness.

The US is initiating alternatives to Mercosur-BRICS cooperation by offering economic incentives or trade benefits to countries in the region that distance themselves from closer cooperation with the BRICS states. This could lead to individual countries reconsidering their positions and withdrawing from cooperation with BRICS.

It is important to emphasize that the countermeasures mentioned are not just hypothetical and that the actual US policy regarding Mercosur-BRICS cooperation depends on many factors, including their strategic interests, developments in the region and the geostrategic situation. Cooperation between the alliances could have various effects on regional and global dynamics and could also potentially lead to tensions and conflicts. In any case, a balanced and constructive cooperation between all actors involved seems desirable in order to promote the stability and sustainable development of the South American region.

The decision of the Mercosur countries to reduce their dependence on the US dollar or to abandon the dollar as a reserve currency could potentially have an impact on the global economic situation and the value of the dollar. While a cautious and strategic approach to monetary policy and trade could help minimize possible risks, such a move would undoubtedly affect the economic and financial landscape in South America and beyond. Close monitoring and a willingness to engage in open dialogue between the countries involved are crucial to ensure the stability and sustainability of global financial markets.

The BRICS Countries and trade with the EU

Until recently, the BRICS and the EU had important trade relations. Trade volumes had been steadily increasing over the past decades, and the EU was one of the largest trading partners for many of the BRICS nations. Raw materials such as oil, coal, precious metals and agricultural products were exported from the BRICS to the EU, while the EU supplied machinery, vehicles, electronics and other products to these emerging markets.

Despite the positive trend in trade relations between the BRICS and the EU, there are also challenges and obstacles that need to be overcome. One of the biggest hurdles is protectionism, which is increasing in some countries in both the EU and the BRICS. Political and financial interests of third parties, as well as trade restrictions and tariffs, affect the free flow of goods and services and make it difficult to achieve optimal trade volumes.

Despite the challenges, trade relations between the BRICS and the EU offered significant opportunities and potential for future growth. Both sides could have benefited from cooperation in the areas of technology, research and development. The BRICS countries have a young and growing population, which creates a large demand for consumer goods and services, while the EU can offer advanced technologies and innovative products.

In addition to pure trade in goods, investments and trade agreements also played a significant role in the relations between the BRICS countries and the EU. Investments enabled companies from both sides to expand into the other's market and benefit from the growth opportunities there. Trade agreements facilitate trade and reduce trade barriers, thereby further strengthening cooperation.

Geopolitical factors play a crucial role in the trade relations of the BRICS countries with the EU. The geopolitical tensions between some BRICS members, especially Russia, China and the EU, affected trade and led to uncertainty. At the same time, constructive cooperation on economic issues could also help to bridge political differences and promote long-term partnerships.

Oil and gas supplies from Russia to the EU played a central role in the trade relations between the two economic areas. Russia is one of the largest producers and exporters of oil and natural gas in the world and covers a significant part of the energy needs of the EU countries. The US dollar, as the reserve currency, has been of great importance in these transactions.

The EU is heavily dependent on energy imports and obtains a significant part of its oil and gas needs from Russia. This energy supply is crucial for the economic stability and development of the EU countries. Countries in Eastern Europe in particular are heavily dependent on Russian energy supplies. This also has geopolitical implications as it increases the EU's energy dependence on Russia. Russia has enormous reserves of oil and natural gas and is therefore a key player in the global energy market. The Russian companies Gazprom and Rosneft are major players in the natural gas and oil industry. The geographical proximity between Russia and the EU facilitates the transport of energy goods via pipelines, which increases the economic viability of these supplies.

Geopolitical tensions between Russia and the EU have in the past led to uncertainty regarding energy supplies and thus economic stability within the EU. Political conflicts have led Russia to use its oil and gas deliveries as a political tool of pressure.

As a BRICS state, Russia has been demanding since 2022 that the ruble be the means of payment for gas from Russia for all EU members. The move away from the US dollar as a transfer currency is part of the BRICS goals.

It is estimated that by then, EU states had spent around $420 million (€380 million) a day on Russian gas and almost $400 million (€362 million) on oil from Russia. These three-digit million amounts in euros or dollars would therefore have to be exchanged for rubles for gas imports alone in order to pay for deliveries.

If the EU were to pay for oil and gas deliveries from Russia in rubles, this could pose significant risks to the dollar as a reserve currency and the associated economic and geopolitical implications.

Since trade in crude oil and natural gas is usually conducted in US dollars, there is strong global demand and dependence on the currency for energy imports. If the EU were to use the ruble instead, it would significantly reduce the demand for US dollars in this particular area as well. This would increase pressure on the dollar and call into question its position as a reserve currency.

Reduced demand for the dollar combined with an increased supply of the currency could lead to a devaluation of the dollar. This would have a negative impact on the US economy as imports would become more expensive and inflation would rise.

The dominance of the dollar as a reserve currency has enabled the US to influence global monetary policy. If other countries, including the EU, were to increasingly use the ruble or the euro, the US could lose its monetary power as it would have less control over global monetary policy.

The dollar has a strong geopolitical component and plays an important role in international relations. By using the dollar in energy transactions, the US has a certain degree of political influence over other countries. If the EU had switched to the ruble as a means of payment, this could reduce the geopolitical importance of the dollar and weaken the international position of the US.

The petrodollar mechanism has evolved over decades and is firmly embedded in global financial markets. A rapid shift from dollars to rubles could lead to disruptions in the international financial system and create uncertainty among investors and markets. A transition by the EU to ruble payments could put economic pressure on the US, prompting it to potentially take countermeasures to defend its interests. This could lead to trade conflicts and further escalate geopolitical tensions.

The EU's switch to ruble payments for oil and gas supplies from Russia would pose significant threats to the dollar and the global financial architecture. The dominance of the dollar as a reserve currency is closely linked to the petrodollar mechanism, and a change in this system could have far-reaching economic and geopolitical implications. It remains to be seen how trade relations and currency practices will develop in the future and how the actors involved will react.

In recent years, there have been discussions about the potential move away from the use of the US dollar in energy transactions. Some countries and companies have started to trade oil and gas in other currencies to reduce their dependence on the dollar and avoid possible US sanctions. If this trend intensifies, it could have a long-term impact on the status of the US dollar as a reserve currency and change the global financial architecture.

Oil and gas supplies from Russia to the EU are of great importance for both economies. Due to its energy dependence on Russia, the EU is striving to diversify its energy sources. At the same time, the US dollar plays a crucial role as a reserve currency in energy transactions and has a significant influence on the global economic structure. The future development of trade relations and the question of the status of the petrodollar are issues that must continue to be closely monitored as they could have far-reaching effects on the international economy.

Trade relations between the BRICS countries and the EU are complex and diverse. They offer both opportunities and challenges that need to be addressed. Increased cooperation, the removal of trade barriers and the promotion of sustainable practices could help to further strengthen relations and create a win-win situation for both sides. As major players in the global economy, the BRICS countries and the EU have the opportunity to work together to contribute to positive economic development and shape a sustainable future. However, the EU's dependence on the US is multifaceted and affects various areas of the economy, politics and security.

The EU and the US are close trading partners and form one of the largest trade relations in the world. Both economies exchange goods and services on a large scale, with the EU recording both exports and imports to the US. A significant part of the EU's trade surplus depends on business with the US, which makes the EU vulnerable to possible trade disputes and protectionist measures by the US.

But security cooperation between the EU and the US is also close and takes place primarily within NATO. The US plays a leading role in NATO. EU countries are largely dependent on US military and strategic support to address challenges such as terrorism, conflict and destabilising developments.

The EU and the US share many common values and interests, which enable close geopolitical alignment. The US dollar has a unique position as a reserve currency and is used as a reserve currency worldwide. This has implications for the international financial system and monetary stability. The EU is somewhat dependent on the dollar's role as a reserve currency, as this influences its own currencies and financial markets.

The US is a leading country in technology and innovation. Many of the world's leading technology companies originnate in the US. The EU depends on US technologies and innovations to remain competitive and drive its economy forward.

The EU is dependent on the US in various areas and these dependencies have far-reaching implications for the EU's economy, security and political direction. The aim should be to develop a balanced and cooperative relationship between the EU and the US to jointly address global challenges and promote a stable and sustainable international order. At the same time, the EU should also work to diversify its dependencies and strengthen its own interests and priorities.

The BRICS Countries and the self-image of the USA

The BRICS countries have become an influential group on the global stage. Their economic strength, population size and geographical location make them significant players in international relations. The USA, on the other hand, is considered one of the world's leading superpowers with deep roots in global affairs. In this chapter, we want to examine the political and economic self-image of the USA and critically examine the relationship between the BRICS countries and the USA.

The USA has a complex trade policy and is known for its international trade. It has concluded numerous bilateral and multilateral trade agreements to promote the free flow of goods and services. At the same time, it has also taken protective measures to protect its own industries and respond to competitors.

The BRICS countries have risen to become an economic and political force in recent decades. With their rapidly growing economies and growing global influence, they aim to question the status quo of international relations and challenge the dominance of the traditional superpowers. This has led to tensions with the USA, especially on issues such as trade and geopolitical interests.

The BRICS countries emphasize their sovereignty and rights as emerging powers demanding a greater voice in international organizations such as the United Nations and the World Bank. They argue that the existing global system does not adequately reflect their interests and needs comprehensive reform.

The economic importance of the BRICS countries cannot be underestimated. Together they represent about 42% of the world's population and about 23% of global gross domestic product. China, as the largest economy among the BRICS countries, has assumed a prominent role in the global economy and is a major trading partner for many countries.

The BRICS countries have also become a major engine of global growth. Their economic rise has attracted many investors and companies seeking to take advantage of the opportunities offered by these emerging markets. The rising middle class in the BRICS countries has also boosted consumption and trade in the region.

The relationship between the BRICS countries and the United States is complex and characterized by competition and cooperation. On the one hand, there are areas in which they have common interests, such as the fight against terrorism and securing the global economy. On the other hand, there are also profound differences of opinion on issues such as trade policy and geopolitical influence.

The US sees the emerging powers of the BRICS countries as a potential challenge to its dominance in the world order. It has concerns about the growing influence of some BRICS countries and the possible impact on its own trade. At the same time, the BRICS countries fear that the US could use its dominance to advance its own interests at the expense of others.

The BRICS countries and the US face a variety of challenges and opportunities in their relations. The economic strength of the BRICS countries and their call for comprehensive reform of the global system have changed the international order and prompted the US to rethink its role in the world.

The path to constructive cooperation lies, among other things, in both sides understanding and respecting each other's interests and values. The US can view the emerging powers as partners who address common global challenges.

To secure its dominance in the world, the United States uses various methods that are political, economic, military and cultural. These methods reflect the pursuit of global dominance and are often referred to as "soft power" and "hard power".

For example, the United States has built an extensive diplomatic network and uses its foreign policy to promote its interests and values worldwide. It is a member of numerous international organizations such as the United Nations, the World Bank and the World Trade Organization (WTO), which provides it with a platform to pursue its political and economic goals. In addition, the United States maintains close relationships with strategic allies and uses its power of influence to forge international alliances.

As the largest economy in the world, the United States uses its economic strength to strengthen its position as a global leader. The US dollar is the world's dominant reserve currency and is used in many international transactions.

The US promotes free trade and invests in foreign markets to increase its influence and secure access to strategically important resources.

In addition, the US has what is probably the strongest military in the world and uses this strength to defend its interests and ensure global security. It maintains military bases around the world and carries out military interventions when necessary to achieve political goals. This has given the US a significant role as the world's policeman, but has also drawn criticism that it uses its military power too heavily.

The US is a technology hub and has a leading role in information technology, space travel, biotechnology and defense technology. This gives the US a competitive advantage in the global economy and contributes to its image as a technological superpower.

The US intelligence and espionage activities are repeatedly criticized when it comes to gathering information, identifying threats and protecting its strategic interests. This includes monitoring communications, cyber operations and covert operations that often remain hidden.

In summary, the US seeks to maintain its dominance in the world through a combination of diplomacy, economic strength, military power, cultural influence, and technological superiority. However, this pursuit of global dominance has also led to controversy and tension with other countries and organizations seeking to protect their own sovereignty and interests. The future development of international relations will depend greatly on the extent to which the US continues to use its methods and how other states respond.

The relationship between the US and the BRICS countries is characterized by complex and often conflicting interests. On the one hand, the US stands as a long-standing superpower and emphasizes its role as a global leader in politics, economics, and security. On the other hand, the BRICS countries have become an influential group on the world stage and demand a fairer distribution of power and resources in the international order, which they also seem willing to defend by any means.

In the economic field, there are both opportunities and challenges in cooperation between the US and the BRICS countries. The BRICS countries have experienced significant economic growth, and their emerging markets offer great opportunities for American companies. At the same time, the United States and the BRICS countries compete in some industries and dispute trade issues and market access.

In security policy, interests are also contradictory. The US has a strong military and a presence in many regions of the world, which has caused distrust among the BRICS countries. The BRICS countries, on the other hand, rely predominantly on their sovereignty and emphasize the right to an independent foreign policy, which is perceived as a challenge to US leadership.

The US places great emphasis on promoting democracy and human rights and sometimes criticizes the domestic affairs of some BRICS countries. The BRICS countries, in turn, see this as interference in their internal affairs and demand respectful cooperation on an equal footing, also recalling past and present actions by the US.

Despite these challenges, there are also areas in which the US and the BRICS countries have common interests and work together, such as combating terrorism, tackling global environmental problems and promoting economic development.

Overall, the relationship between the US and the BRICS countries reflects the dynamic changes in the global order. While the US seeks to maintain its dominance in the world and emphasizes its traditional role as a leading power, the BRICS countries are calling for a more equitable and multipolar world order that reflects their growing importance. As recent events show, they too are determined to support their influence and interests militarily.

The future of the relationship between the US and the BRICS countries will depend on the ability of both sides to understand each other's interests, make compromises and find constructive solutions. The challenges and opportunities in this relationship will also be significantly influenced by global developments, political interactions and efforts to achieve multilateral cooperation. The international community will be called upon to bridge the differences between the US and the BRICS countries and find ways to shape a cooperative and stable world order that meets the interests of all countries.

Afrexim Bank, the US Dollar and the BRICS

The African Export-Import Bank, also known as Afrexim Bank, is a continental financial institution that has played an increasingly important role in the African economy and trade landscape over the past few decades. Established in 1993, it has grown into one of the largest multilateral banks focused on promoting and supporting trade within Africa and between Africa and other regions of the world.

Its primary focus is on financing trade deals and projects designed to drive economic growth on the African continent. The bank has a wide range of financial products and services, including trade finance, project finance, export credit, payment protection and payment guarantees. In doing so, Afrexim Bank works closely with other international financial institutions as well as governments and companies.

A crucial factor in Afrexim Bank's operations is the use of currencies for trade and project financing. Historically, the US dollar has been the dominant currency in global trade, and in Africa too, the dollar has been the dominant reserve currency. However, the use of the US dollar in international trade also presents some challenges and risks for African countries.

With the rise of the BRICS countries and their increasing economic importance, the dynamics in global trade have changed. The BRICS countries have taken an important role in shaping the global economic agenda and have also established their own development bank, the New

Development Bank, to finance infrastructure projects in developing and emerging economies.

These developments have led to some African countries starting to increasingly conduct their trade relations and financing in the currencies of the BRICS countries. This trend has been supported by the Afrexim Bank, which has been actively working to promote the use of BRICS currencies in Africa's trade. This is intended to reduce dependence on the US dollar and strengthen the stability and resilience of African economies.

The BRICS countries also have an interest in strengthening their currencies in international trade and reducing the influence of the US dollar. China, as the leading economy within the BRICS, has in particular made great efforts to establish the renminbi (RMB) as an international reserve currency and to promote the use of RMB in global trade.

For Afrexim Bank and African countries, the increased use of BRICS currencies in trade and financing offers several advantages. Firstly, currencies such as the renminbi, the Russian ruble or the Brazilian real can be more stable than the US dollar, which is often subject to fluctuations. This can make trade and financing operations for African companies less vulnerable to exchange rate fluctuations.

In addition, the use of BRICS currencies in trade with the countries concerned can strengthen trade relations and facilitate access to new markets. The BRICS countries have a wide range of goods and services to offer that may be of interest to African countries, and the use of their currencies can facilitate trade in these areas.

Afrexim Bank has also developed programs to encourage and support commercial banks in Africa to conduct trade finance and projects in BRICS currencies. This includes training for bank staff and providing financial instruments that facilitate the use of BRICS currencies.

However, there are also challenges to increasing the use of BRICS currencies in trade and finance in Africa. One of these is the limited liquidity and availability of BRICS currencies in international financial markets. The US dollar remains the most widely used and accepted currency globally and it can be difficult for African companies to obtain sufficient BRICS currencies for their trade transactions.

Another obstacle is the familiarity and trust of actors in the African trading system with the US dollar. The dollar has built a solid foundation of trust over many years and is still the preferred currency for international transactions. The move to BRICS currencies therefore requires a change in mindset and an understanding of the new dynamics in the trading system.

Despite these challenges, some African countries have begun to diversify their reserves and hold more in BRICS currencies to reduce their dependence on the US dollar.

Afrexim Bank plays a critical role in supporting these diversification efforts and promoting greater integration of Africa into the global economy.

The collaboration between Afrexim Bank and the BRICS countries is expected to continue to grow in the coming years, creating new opportunities for trade and investment on the African continent. The Bank will continue to expand its role as a catalyst for growth and development in Africa, playing a crucial role in promoting trade, industrialization and economic diversification.

Overall, Afrexim Bank has a remarkable track record in supporting African economies, empowering numerous companies to enter new markets and expand their manufacturing capacity through its trade finance and project lending.

Looking ahead, Afrexim Bank sees further opportunities and challenges. One of the key challenges is to continue to develop and modernize infrastructure in Africa. Infrastructure projects are critical to facilitate trade within the continent and better connect Africa with the rest of the world. Afrexim Bank can play a significant role in this by providing financing for such projects and contributing its expertise in project development and implementation.

Another important aspect is promoting regional integration in Africa. The continent is diverse and different in many ways, but it is precisely through increased cooperation and trade between African countries that synergies can be created. Afrexim Bank has already launched various initiatives to promote regional integration, including the creation of trade corridors and supporting companies that operate across borders.

In terms of the use of currencies in trade, the US dollar still plays a dominant role, but Afrexim Bank and African countries are actively working to reduce dependence on this one currency. Promoting the use of BRICS currencies and other stable currencies can help increase resilience to external shocks and open up a wider variety of trading partners for African companies.

Another important development is the trend towards digitalization and the role of digital currencies. Cryptocurrencies and digital payment systems are gaining traction around the world, and innovative solutions that can facilitate trade and financing are also emerging in Africa. Afrexim Bank has recognized the potential of digitalization and is working to leverage new technologies to give African companies access to modern and efficient payment systems.

In addition to its economic importance, Afrexim Bank also has an important social component. It is actively committed to promoting sustainable development and social responsibility in Africa. Through various initiatives, it supports programs to combat poverty, promote education and strengthen social infrastructure. The bank is aware that sustainable economic development is inextricably linked to social and environmental aspects.

Afrexim Bank also has a strong partnership with other international organizations, including the World Bank, the African Development Bank and the United Nations. This cooperation enables the bank to expand its resources and expertise and increase its impact on the African continent.

Overall, Afrexim Bank plays a significant role in promoting trade and economic development in Africa. Its initiatives and programs help strengthen African economies and facilitate trade with other regions of the world. Engaging with the BRICS countries and promoting the use of BRICS currencies are part of its strategy to reduce dependence on the US dollar and drive Africa's economic diversification.

Looking ahead, Afrexim Bank will continue to play an important role in supporting economic development and promoting trade in Africa. Its ability to adapt to new challenges and develop innovative solutions will be crucial to accompany African economies on their path to sustainable growth and prosperity.

The African Export-Import Bank has taken an ambivalent attitude towards the US dollar. Historically, the dollar has been the dominant reserve currency and the main means of international trade. In this regard, Afrexim Bank undoubtedly recognizes the importance of the dollar as a widely used currency.

However, Afrexim Bank is also aware of the challenges that come with over-dependence on the US dollar. For African countries in particular, this dependence can lead to risks in times of exchange rate fluctuations and economic turmoil. The Bank is therefore actively pursuing a policy of diversifying foreign exchange reserves and promoting alternative currencies for trade and financing in Africa.

Afrexim Bank has been working harder in recent years to promote the use of BRICS currencies in African trade. It recognises the potential of these currencies, which are often more stable than the US dollar, and sees this as an opportunity to strengthen the resilience of African economies.

By promoting trade transactions in BRICS currencies, Afrexim Bank offers African companies the opportunity to reduce their dependence on the US dollar and instead trade in currencies that are also gaining traction in other emerging economies. This can help strengthen trade relations between Africa and the BRICS countries and open up new opportunities for trade and investment.

In addition, Afrexim Bank also has a particular interest in promoting the use of digital currencies and innovative payment systems. It recognizes the potential of these new technologies to make trade and finance in Africa more efficient and secure. The Bank has developed programs and initiatives to promote the acceptance and use of digital currencies in the African economy.

Overall, the African Export-Import Bank has a pragmatic attitude towards the US dollar. It recognises the importance of the dollar as the dominant reserve currency and for global trade. At the same time, it actively seeks to diversify foreign exchange reserves and promote alternative currencies, particularly BRICS currencies, in order to reduce dependence on the dollar and strengthen economic stability in Africa.

The outlook for the US Dollar and the BRICS Countries

The global economy and international trade depend on various factors and currencies. For many decades, the US dollar has played a prominent role as a reserve currency, controlling the international financial system. But in recent years, the BRICS countries have increasingly emerged as economic and political actors and adversaries, raising questions about whether dollar dominance will last in the long term.

The development of the BRICS countries has changed the global power structure. These emerging economies have large populations, natural resources, a rapidly growing middle class, and increasing technological capacity. China in particular, the largest member of the BRICS countries, has experienced tremendous economic expansion, becoming the second largest economy in the world. This dynamic has led the BRICS countries to want to exercise more political influence at the international level and to seek a larger role in the global monetary system.

One challenge to dollar dominance is the dependence of many countries on the United States as a trading partner and debtor. In recent years, however, the BRICS countries have strengthened their economic ties with each other and have increasingly concluded bilateral trade agreements. China in particular has expanded its trade links with Russia, Brazil and India and intensified cooperation in areas such as energy, infrastructure and technology. This increased cooperation reduces dependence on Western economies and opens up new opportunities for the BRICS countries to bring their own currencies into international trade.

Another factor influencing the prospects for dollar dominance is the digitization of the financial system. Cryptocurrencies such as Bitcoin have gained importance in recent years and could potentially represent an alternative to traditional currencies. Some countries, including members of the BRICS countries, have already taken steps to develop their own digital currencies. In the long term, this could lead to a fragmentation of the global monetary system and challenge the dominance of the US dollar.

Despite these developments, dollar dominance is unlikely to be completely replaced any time soon. The US dollar remains the most widely used reserve currency and is viewed as a safe investment in many countries. The US economy remains strong and the US dollar is used in many international transactions. In addition, the US dollar has a well-established financial system and extensive infrastructure that other currencies have yet to develop.

While the BRICS countries have the potential to transform the international financial system, they also face challenges of their own. For example, some of these countries struggle with economic imbalances, corruption and political instability. These factors could affect their economic development and limit their ambitions in the global monetary system.

Overall, the prospects for dollar dominance and the BRICS countries depend on a variety of factors. The BRICS countries are expected to continue to strengthen their position and influence the international financial system. At the same time, the US dollar is expected to maintain its leading role as a reserve currency, at least for now. It is possible that the global monetary system will include several reserve currencies in the future, but the US dollar will play an important role.

It remains to be seen how the geopolitical landscape evolves and what actions the BRICS countries take to realize their ambitions in the international financial system. Close monitoring of economic and political developments in the BRICS countries and their impact on the global economy will be of great importance to understand the future dynamics between dollar dominance and the BRICS countries.

One important aspect that influences the prospects for dollar dominance and the BRICS countries is commodity trade. Many of the BRICS countries are rich in natural resources such as oil, gas, metals and agricultural products. The global demand for these commodities will continue to rise, giving the BRICS countries the opportunity to diversify their exports and strengthen their currencies in this area. At the same time, the BRICS countries are striving to reduce their dependence on dollar denomination in commodity trade by using direct currency swaps and bilateral trade agreements.

Another crucial factor is the role of international financial institutions. Historically, institutions such as the International Monetary Fund (IMF) and the World Bank have been dominated by the western developed countries, especially the US. This has made the BRICS countries feel that their voices and interests are not adequately represented. Therefore, they have pushed for the establishment of their own financial institutions such as the New

Development Bank (NDB) and the Asian Infrastructure Investment Bank (AIIB). These new institutions provide a platform for the BRICS countries to further their economic and political goals and reduce dependence on the established institutions.

However, the challenges to dollar dominance and the ambitions of the BRICS countries are many. The stability of the global financial system and the trustworthiness of a currency depend on various factors including economic performance, political stability, legal certainty and the independence of the central bank. Although the BRICS countries have made progress in many of these areas, there are still areas where improvements are needed.

Another crucial factor is public perception and trust in a currency. The US dollar is viewed as a safe currency around the world, which is due to the stability and depth of the US financial market and the political and economic power of the United States. The BRICS countries have yet to develop the same level of trust in their currencies, especially when it comes to investing large amounts of wealth or conducting international business.

The geopolitical dynamics between the US and the BRICS countries also play a role. In recent years, there have been tensions and conflicts in various areas, be it trade disputes, geopolitical tensions or political differences. These geopolitical challenges can affect the efforts of the BRICS countries to strengthen their currencies and their position in the international financial system.

Despite the challenges, there are also opportunities for closer cooperation between the US and the BRICS countries. Increased cooperation in areas such as trade, investment, technology exchange and development cooperation could lead to a positive interaction and increase mutual trust. A constructive partnership between the US and the BRICS could help improve the stability of the global financial system and strengthen prospects for both sides.

In summary, the prospects for dollar dominance and the BRICS are closely interrelated and influenced by a variety of factors. The BRICS undoubtedly have the potential to transform the international financial system and strengthen their currencies. At the same time, the US dollar continues to be the leading reserve currency and the economic and political power of the US plays a crucial role. The future will show how relations between the US and the BRICS develop and whether the global monetary system moves towards a multipolar order in which multiple currencies play a significant role. It remains exciting to observe these developments and analyze their impact on the global economy.

The prospects for dollar dominance and the BRICS can also be influenced by external events and global trends. One example of this is the current debate about climate change and the need for sustainable development. The BRICS countries have a significant impact on global carbon emissions and energy consumption. If they jointly commit to a low-carbon economy and develop their renewable energy capacities, this could not only boost their own economic development but also enhance their international standing and position their currencies as environmentally friendly alternatives.

Another factor affecting the prospects for dollar dominance and the BRICS countries is the growing digitization and rise of new technologies. The BRICS countries have recognized that innovation and technology are a critical driver of economic growth and competitiveness. Therefore, they have made increased efforts to build their technological capacities and invest in areas such as artificial intelligence, digital infrastructure, e-commerce and fintech. By using modern technologies, the BRICS countries could create new trade routes and payment systems that reduce dependence on the US dollar and strengthen their own currencies.

A key trend affecting the prospects for dollar dominance is the increasing regionalization of trade. In recent years, many countries have entered into trade agreements at the regional level to facilitate access to markets and promote economic integration. The BRICS countries have played an active role here as well. For example, they have pushed for the formation of the BRICS Single Market to facilitate trade and investment among members. Through regional trade agreements, the BRICS countries can strengthen their economic ties and position their currencies as preferred means of payment in these regional blocs.

However, it is important to note that the issue of dollar dominance and the prospects for the BRICS countries is not determined solely by the BRICS countries themselves. The role of the US and other global players is crucial. US policies regarding the dollar, trade sanctions, financial regulation and geopolitical relations will undoubtedly impact the prospects for dollar dominance and the BRICS countries.

In summary, the prospects for dollar dominance and the BRICS depend on a variety of factors, including economic performance, political stability, regional integration, technological development, and external events. The BRICS undoubtedly have the potential to transform the international financial system and strengthen their own currencies. At the same time, the US dollar remains a significant reserve currency accepted by many countries around the world. Time will tell how the geopolitical landscape evolves and how the BRICS realize their ambitions in the global monetary system. Close monitoring of economic and political developments in the BRICS as well as international financial markets will be crucial to understanding the future dynamics between dollar dominance and the BRICS.

Closing words

Given the rapid changes in the global economic landscape and the ongoing debate about the dominance of the dollar and the rise of the BRICS, it is crucial to reflect on the developments of the past few years and consider possible future scenarios.

This book has attempted to shed light on the factors that have shaped the dominance of the dollar as the world's reserve currency and to analyze the dynamics that are helping the BRICS countries establish themselves as emerging economic powers. We have looked at the historical backgrounds, economic strengths and weaknesses, and political ambitions of these countries to paint a comprehensive picture.

It is important to note, however, that the future of dollar dominance and the BRICS countries is by no means predetermined. The challenges facing both the dollar and the BRICS countries are manifold. The US must maintain its economic competitiveness and get its high level of debt under control to ensure the stability of the dollar in the long term. At the same time, the BRICS countries have to deal with the internal challenges of economic development and political stability.

The future will undoubtedly depend on the ability of the BRICS countries to strengthen their cooperation and use their economic potentials. It is not excluded that they will play a greater role in the global financial world in the coming years. Nevertheless, it is unlikely that the dollar will give up its dominant position in the near future. The long-standing basis of trust and the wide acceptance of the dollar in international trade are difficult to shake.

The future is always uncertain and it remains difficult to make predictions. Nevertheless, some possible scenarios can be foreseen in the battle for the supremacy of the US dollar against the BRICS countries. The BRICS countries could gradually settle their international transactions in their regional currencies in order to strengthen their economic independence and break away from dependence on the US dollar. This could lead to the dollar losing influence in the world.

Prolonged economic weakness or instability in the US can shake confidence in the dollar and favor other currencies, including those of the BRICS countries.

The BRICS countries can create their own reserve currency based on real gold reserves to position themselves jointly against the US dollar. However, this would pose significant challenges, as the US will not give up its leadership positions without a fight. Given the current political and military events in the world, it is expected that these confrontations will lead to significant disruptions in the financial and political systems.

Geopolitical shifts can affect the status of the dollar. For example, political conflicts or trade wars can weaken the dollar and the BRICS countries may rely more on their regional currencies.

The development depends on numerous factors, including economic, political and geostrategic developments by the US, the BRICS countries and in the overall global situation.

Both sides are currently showing that they do not shy away from asserting their own interests, even by military means if necessary. This shows once again how tense the global situation is and how important joint discussions are in order to prevent such conflicts from escalating into a military global conflict, but to resolve them diplomatically at bilateral levels.

However, this requires the willingness and ability of the actors. The aim must be in everyone's interest to stop the military actions and replace them with negotiations that lead to a common solution.

It is important that we carefully observe current developments and understand the impact on global society. Through dialogue and the exchange of ideas, we can work together to create a better future for all countries and regions.

Thank you for following along with this book. May the insights and discussions presented here contribute to a deeper understanding of the complex world of finance and the emerging BRICS states.

Hermann Selchow

www.ingramcontent.com/pod-product-compliance
Lightning Source LLC
LaVergne TN
LVHW090315210926
848480LV00001B/253
* 9 7 9 8 2 2 7 1 1 8 4 3 1 *